Outcomes-focused services for older people

Caroline Glendinning, Sue Clarke, Phillipa Hare,
Inna Kotchetkova, Jane Maddison and Liz Newbronner

First published in Great Britain in December 2006
by the Social Care Institute for Excellence

Written by Caroline Glendinning, Sue Clarke, Phillipa Hare,
Inna Kotchetkova, Jane Maddison and Liz Newbronner

ISBN-10 1-904812-33-3
ISBN-13 978-1-904812-33-3

Produced by The Policy Press
Fourth Floor, Beacon House
Queen's Road
Bristol BS8 1QU
tel 0117 331 4054
fax 0117 331 4093
tpp-info@bristol.ac.uk
www.policypress.org.uk

**This report is available in print and online
www.scie.org.uk**

Social Care Institute for Excellence
Goldings House
2 Hay's Lane
London SE1 2HB
tel 020 7089 6840
fax 020 7089 6841
textphone 020 7089 6893
www.scie.org.uk

Contents

Executive summary   v

1   Research review   1
  1.1   Introduction to research review   1
  1.2   Definitions: what are 'outcomes'?   2
  1.3   What outcomes do older people value?   3
      1.3.1 Change outcomes   3
      1.3.2 Maintenance or prevention outcomes   4
      1.3.3 Process outcomes   6
      1.3.4 Outcomes and diversity   8
      1.3.5 Views of the User Advisory Group   9
  1.4   Organisational arrangements impeding   9
      outcomes-focused services
      1.4.1 Introduction   9
      1.4.2 Assessment   10
      1.4.3 Reviews   11
      1.4.4 Purchasing of care 'packages'   12
      1.4.5 Provider-level barriers   13
      1.4.6 Role of commissioners   14
      1.4.7 Importance of communication   15
      1.4.8 Impact of the health–social care divide   16
      1.4.9 Barriers and diversity   17
      1.4.10 Views of the User Advisory Group   17
  1.5   Organisational arrangements facilitating   18
      outcomes-focused services
      1.5.1 Introduction   18
      1.5.2 Assessment   18
      1.5.3 Reviews   19
      1.5.4 Micro-level commissioning of care   21
           'packages'
      1.5.5 Provider-level factors   21
      1.5.6 Importance of communication   22
      1.5.7 Overcoming the health–social care divide   22
      1.5.8 Initiatives and diversity   23
      1.5.9 Views of the User Advisory Group   23
  1.6   Conclusions of research review   24

2   Practice survey   25
     2.1   Introduction to practice survey   25
     2.2   Postal survey   26
           2.2.1 Aims   26
           2.2.2 Methods   27
           2.2.3 Respondent characteristics   27
           2.2.4 Nature and range of outcomes work   28
           2.2.5 Achievements and factors helping and   33
                  hindering achievements
           2.2.6 Postal survey: discussion   38
     2.3   Case studies   39
           2.3.1 Introduction   39
           2.3.2 Outcomes-focused activities   41
           2.3.3 Outcomes-focused services   47
           2.3.4 Monitoring and evaluation   48
           2.3.5 Impact of outcomes-focused services: 50
                  the experiences of service users
           2.3.6 Factors facilitating outcomes approaches   54
           2.3.7 What hinders outcomes approaches?   57
           2.3.8 Plans for (further) outcomes-focused   59
                  service developments

3   Conclusions   63

     References   67

     Appendix 1: User involvement in the knowledge   75
     review

     Appendix 2: Methods used in the knowledge review   83

     Appendix 3: Summary of case study sites: services   93
     and activities

     Appendix 4: Data collection and project documents   99

     Appendix 5: Information about SPRU and   127
     Acton Shapiro

     Index   129

Executive summary

Introduction to research review

This knowledge review includes:

- a review of research evidence on the outcomes valued by older people and the factors that facilitate and inhibit achieving these outcomes
- a postal survey of localities and social services managers in England and Wales known to be interested in developing outcomes-focused approaches to older people's services; and in-depth studies in six localities. This was supplemented by information supplied by members of the Outcomes Network (originally established by SPRU and now supported by the DH Change Agent Team's Better Commissioning Learning and Information Network).

The knowledge review was supported by a user advisory group of six older service users who met three times during the project.

Definitions

'Outcomes' refer to the impacts or end results of services on a person's life. Outcomes-focused services therefore aim to achieve the aspirations, goals and priorities identified by service users – in contrast to services whose content and/or forms of delivery are standardised or are determined solely by those who deliver them. Outcomes are by definition individualised, as they depend on the priorities and aspirations of individual people.

Research into the outcomes valued by older people

Three groups of social care service outcomes have been identified; these are very similar to the factors that older people identify as central to their independence and well-being:

Outcomes involving change

- Improvements in physical symptoms and behaviour.
- Improvements in physical functioning and mobility.
- Improvements in morale.

Outcomes involving maintenance or prevention

- Meeting basic physical needs.
- Ensuring personal safety and security.
- Having a clean and tidy home environment.
- Keeping alert and active.
- Having social contact and company, including opportunities to contribute as well as receive help.
- Having control over daily routines.

Service process outcomes

These refer to the ways that services are accessed and delivered and include:

- Feeling valued and respected.
- Being treated as an individual.
- Having a say and control over services.
- Value for money.
- A good 'fit' with other sources of support.
- Compatibility with, and respect for, cultural and religious preferences.

The limited research evidence indicates that older people from ethnic minority communities and with different types of impairments value the same broad range of outcomes. However the priority assigned to different outcomes may vary according to age, living circumstances and type of impairment.

Research into factors facilitating and inhibiting outcomes-focused services for older people

Research shows that a number of factors relating to the operation of social care quasi-markets may affect the delivery of outcomes-focused services.

Assessment, care planning and review

- Service-led assessments that do not offer choice.
- Assessments that emphasise dependency or overlook psychological and emotional needs.
- Assessments that do not challenge low expectations of services or the limited range of help older people think it legitimate to request.
- Fragmented or irregular reviews of service users.
- The health and social care divide, where this prevents holistic assessment and care planning.

Micro-level purchasing

How care managers purchase services from providers of home care services has a major impact on the delivery of outcomes-focused services. Purchasing specified periods of time or help with specified tasks can restrict both the flexibility and personalisation of services; purchasing just enough time (or tasks) to maintain physical well-being can threaten change and process outcomes, as well as maintenance outcomes relating to social participation.

Provider-level barriers

Difficulty recruiting and retaining staff reduces the flexibility of providers to provide individualised services, even where older people are willing to purchase (extra) services privately. Levels of funding from social services purchasers can restrict providers' opportunities to offer fair working conditions and training and thus attract and retain good quality staff.

Commissioning and contracting

Commissioning and contracting arrangements exert major influences over the delivery of outcomes-focused services, particularly by independent sector (rather than in-house) providers. Contracts allowing providers to vary the price they charge purchasers offer incentives to respond to individual priorities and needs.

Within quasi-markets, communication is vital to outcomes-focused services. This includes communication between:

- care managers, contracts managers and providers, so that contracts reflect users' needs and preferences.
- providers and care managers, about changes in users' priorities and circumstances.
- users, front-line staff, provider managers and purchasers, so that changes in needs are quickly identified and any service changes implemented.

In addition, front-line staff in regular contact with older people need to be well-equipped with up-to-date information about other services outside their immediate area of expertise.

Research evidence on initiatives promoting outcomes-focused services

Researched development projects conducted by the Social Policy Research Unit, University of York have tested with social services partners ways of introducing outcomes-focused approaches into routine social care practice. Using appropriately designed documentation to shape front-line practice, the following approaches have been successfully implemented:

- Identifying and summarising older people's desired outcomes during assessment.
- Briefing home care staff on older people's desired outcomes.
- Identifying outcomes for carers during assessments and reviews.
- Using postal questionnaires to collect information on outcomes.

In addition, direct payments have been shown to enable older people to achieve desired outcomes. However, this success appears to depend on the availability of local support (formal or informal) to manage direct payments; take-up among older people remains low.

Practice survey I: Postal survey

A postal survey aimed to establish the range and extensiveness of outcomes-focused developments in older people's social care services across England and Wales. Following careful screening of existing contacts, at least 70 such initiatives were identified. Social services were generally the sole or lead agency; the most common partners were NHS primary care trusts and private service providers. Significantly, most initiatives were described as currently being planned, piloted or 'rolled out'; only 17 per cent had been established for up to three years and only 13 per cent for three-plus years.

Outcomes-focused initiatives were most likely to involve services for older people living at home and/or following hospital discharge. Initiatives included developing outcomes approaches in assessment, care planning and review; changing existing services and commissioning new ones; and monitoring to see how far services meet user outcomes. Only moderate levels of user involvement in planning these initiatives were reported.

Because so many of the reported initiatives were still at an early stage, some respondents thought it was too early to judge whether they were successful; those who were able to generally judged them to be partly or fully successful. However, given the constraints of a postal survey, it was not possible to know what success criteria were being used or how far these judgements reflected the experiences of older people using outcomes-focused services.

Respondents also identified a number of factors that helped and hindered progress in developing outcomes-focused approaches, and cited measures to overcome these barriers. These factors were explored in in-depth case studies.

Practice survey II: In-depth case studies

Six localities where outcomes-focused approaches were well established were selected from responses to the postal survey. They covered a range of activities (assessment, care planning and review, commissioning and contracting for new and existing services); and services (day care, intermediate care, prevention services, community-based rehabilitation, home care and residential care). Additional examples were obtained from members of the former SPRU Outcomes network.

Outcomes-focused activities

Assessment, care planning and review

Sites that had developed outcomes-focused approaches had found them difficult to integrate with the Single Assessment Process. However a number of ways had been found to incorporate outcomes into care planning; these could also form the basis of reviews.

Commissioning for change outcomes

Localities had recently established intermediate care services jointly with NHS partners; some had also restructured their in-house home care services to provide short-term reablement services to all new users, free of charge. Desired outcomes (for example, being able to manage housework or walk to the shops) were identified during assessments. Care and rehabilitation staff had considerable autonomy over how they worked with older people to achieve these outcomes. Rebuilding confidence and morale was considered as important as – and underpinned – improvements in physical functioning.

Commissioning for maintenance outcomes

Three sites had amended contracts with independent home care providers to facilitate more flexible, outcomes-focused services. Changes included:

- establishing 'zones' for each provider, thus reducing staff travel time

- agreeing in advance estimated workloads and payments, with providers billing retrospectively for actual time spent
- building spare time into contracts for providers to use flexibly to meet additional requests from users, free of charge.

These changes were expected to provide flexibility for unexpected emergencies; guarantee staff minimum weekly hours; allow staff to be employed on a shift basis; and offer opportunities for staff training. Only one such change in contracting had been evaluated: higher levels of user satisfaction and increased job satisfaction by front-line staff were reported; only eight per cent of care packages exceeded their estimated budget.

These changes involve transferring power and responsibility from purchasers to providers and users. They require high levels of trust, open communication channels and appropriate performance and financial management systems.

Two sites had recently commissioned low level preventive services from Age Concern and other voluntary organisations – these included shopping, home visiting and social activities.

Outcomes-focused services

Intermediate care and reablement services
These were areas where staff thought they had made most progress in establishing outcomes-focused services. Services offered a holistic approach, tailored to meeting individual goals; progress towards these could be easily monitored. Users confirmed these outcomes.

Day care
Users valued outcomes-focused day services that identified their interests and linked them to staff with similar interests. Ethnic minority users valued day services employing staff who spoke their languages.

Residential care
A local quality development scheme for nursing and residential homes encouraged individualised service user plans and placed heavy emphasis on maximising choice, control and independence that contributed to maintenance and process outcomes.

Monitoring and evaluation

Systematic and routine monitoring, often using clinical tools, was common in reablement and intermediate care services. There was less evidence of routine outcome monitoring among users of longer-term home care services.

Factors facilitating outcomes-focused approaches

These included:

- national policies such as the National Service Framework for older people and the Green Paper on adult social care
- local vision, leadership and investment in change management, including staff induction and regular training workshops
- partnerships and whole-systems working; these helped secure access to resources and skills that were essential to user outcomes but located outside the remit of social care
- new investments in intermediate care services involving user-led care outcomes. Establishing new services also enabled outcomes-focused culture and practice to be established from the start
- bidding for Partnerships for Older People Projects that would allow investment in preventive services to meet desired maintenance outcomes

Factors hindering outcomes-focused approaches

These included:

- Single Assessment Process
- other national policies, inspection regimes and performance indicators
- resource constraints
- staff culture and attitudes at all levels
- user and carer attitudes.

Older people's perspectives

Older people interviewed in the practice survey confirmed the very significant benefits of intermediate care and reablement services aimed at achieving change outcomes. Users of these services affirmed how they had been encouraged to identify important goals and helped to achieve these. They reported significant improvements in confidence and morale as well as physical functioning. These improvements were attributed to the fact that these services were delivered in ways that maximised users' choice and control.

Older people using residential and day care services also confirmed the process outcomes of highly individualised care. However, it was difficult to find examples of holistic approaches in which services met a wide range of desired maintenance outcomes.

The User Advisory Group confirmed the importance of services responding to individual needs and differences; of choice and control over services; and of help with low level tasks such as cleaning, gardening and shopping. The Group highlighted the difficulties experienced by some older people, particularly from ethnic minority communities, in accessing services without additional support. Voluntary organisations and NHS services, particularly GPs, were thought to have important roles to play in helping older people access services and achieve desired outcomes. Voluntary organisations can also provide information and advocacy for older people who are isolated or find it hard to access services.

Conclusions

Although recent policies have emphasised outcomes-focused services, in some localities such approaches have been in operation for some time. SPRU's Outcomes programme, with its associated training and development material, enabled some localities to make significant developments, particularly in outcomes-focused approaches to assessment, care planning and review.

More recently, targeted funding and performance indicators related to hospital admission and discharge have given a significant impetus to the development of services focused on change outcomes, both in collaboration with NHS partners and by local authority in-house services.

However, in general, there remains a significant disjunction between these developments and the capacity of independent home care services to deliver long-term maintenance and process outcomes. Some localities are building on the conclusions of extensive research into care management and commissioning within social care quasi-markets and are developing less rigid and bureaucratic approaches to commissioning and purchasing services, particularly from independent home care providers. The impact of these new approaches on users' experiences needs thorough and systematic evaluation.

Resource constraints and poor relationships with independent providers in other areas continue to impede the introduction of more flexible, individualised home care services.

The emergent policy emphasis on prevention means that efforts are being made to develop low-level preventive services, often through partnerships with local voluntary and community organisations. These may contribute to valued maintenance outcomes such as domestic help and social participation. The Partnerships for Older People Projects will provide valuable evidence in the future about the effectiveness of these approaches to meeting desired outcomes.

Three broader issues remain. First, although this knowledge review found many examples of high quality, outcome-oriented services, these were often fragmented and service-specific. For example, the outcomes focus of reablement services was often not carried through into long-term home care services. Similarly, good quality day services addressed maintenance and process outcomes, but there was little support for maintaining these outcomes outside the day centre.

Secondly, the concept and practice of 'outcomes' is subject to multiple interpretations and disciplinary perspectives. Some services had a strong outcomes focus as a consequence of other policies, such as the development of intermediate care and reablement services, or new approaches to the inspection of residential care. The concept and practice of outcomes mapped most readily onto intermediate care and reablement services. However, even here, GPs and clinicians were reported sometimes not to understand the concept of outcomes, with consequences for the appropriateness of their referrals and advice to older patients. Moreover, many intermediate care services screen potential users carefully and admit only those able to achieve change outcomes. This risks equating 'outcomes' with 'change outcomes'. Longer-term maintenance and prevention outcomes, and groups of older people such as those with dementia for whom maintenance, prevention and process outcomes are especially important, consequently risk being marginalised. 'Flexible', 'person-centred' or 'responsive' may be more appropriate and inclusive terms than 'outcome'.

Third, as the user advisory group confirmed, many of the outcomes desired by older people do not, on the face of it, appear to be derived from interventions that currently fall within the remit of social care services. Partnerships with other statutory and voluntary agencies will be necessary to support older people, for example, in keeping alert and active, continuing to participate in social networks and other maintenance and preventive outcomes. A 'whole systems' approach to the commissioning, review and evaluation of outcomes-focused services is therefore essential.

Research review

1.1 Introduction to research review

The Social Care Institute for Excellence (SCIE) commissioned the Social Policy Research Unit (SPRU) at the University of York to undertake a knowledge review on outcomes-focused services for older people. The knowledge review consists of:

- a review of research on outcomes and outcomes-focused services
- a national survey and case study examples of current and emerging approaches to commissioning and delivering outcomes-focused services for older people across England and Wales.

A User Advisory Group was established to guide the knowledge review (*see* Appendix 1).

The research review aims to:

- summarise research on the outcomes that older people value and wish to achieve from contact with social care services
- identify factors that facilitate or inhibit outcomes-focused services.

Details of how the research review was conducted are contained in Appendix 2. Research included in the review was mainly conducted before a number of important measures, likely to have impacted on policy and practice, were implemented. Thus the impact of partnership working as promoted by Section 31 of the Health Act 1999, the National Service Framework (NSF) for older people, the Single Assessment Process (SAP), Fair Access to Care Services (FACS) guidance and measures to promote the take-up of direct payments by older people may serve to modify some of the conclusions of the review. However, evidence of their effects in promoting outcomes-focused services is not yet available.

1.2 Definitions: what are 'outcomes'?

For the purposes of this review, 'outcomes' refer to *the impacts or end results of services on a person's life*. Outcomes-focused services are therefore those that aim to achieve the goals, aspirations or priorities of individual service users. They can be contrasted with services whose content and/or form of delivery are standardised, regardless of the circumstances of users; and with services whose goals, content and mode of delivery are primarily determined by those who commission or deliver them rather than those who use them.

The concept of 'outcomes' is closely related to that of 'quality of life'. There is a high degree of consistency between different studies in the outcomes that are valued by older people; these also relate closely to factors that older people have identified as contributing to 'quality of life'.

Recently the term 'personalisation' has begun to be used.[1] Personalisation includes the tailoring of services to fit individual aspirations and priorities; and the active participation of service users in the processes of designing and delivering services: '... by putting users at the heart of services, enabling them to become participants in the design and delivery, services will be more effective by mobilising millions of people as co-producers of the public goods they value' [1, pp 17–19]. This approach is also reflected in proposals contained in the adult social care Green Paper[2] and the government-wide strategy on ageing.[3]

Research into experiences of 'personalising' services, as defined above, is as yet very limited; an evidence base is urgently needed.[2] However, as will be shown below, the importance of having a say in how services are delivered is an important 'process outcome' for older people, so much of the research reviewed in the first part of this report will also be relevant to the development of 'personalised' services.

Another closely related concept is that of 'independence'.[4–6] Again, considerable overlaps exist between commonly desired or valued outcomes and the dimensions of independence identified by older people. Indeed, it would be perverse if social care services did *not* contribute to outcomes that are consistent with the dimensions of independence as defined by older people. Moreover, older people who anticipate service outcomes that are incompatible with their concepts of independence are likely to reject services and try to find other ways of meeting their needs.[7]

This review aimed to identify research on the outcomes that older people aspire to achieve from social care services. However, many of these outcomes do not, on the face of it, appear to be directly related to the bulk of current social care services for older people – home care, day care and residential care. Indeed, research shows how older people have broad, holistic perspectives on desired outcomes and may expect social care services to contribute to achieving these.[8] This holistic perspective is congruent with the Green Paper on adult social care[2] and therefore with the shift in practice that will be required to implement the Green Paper proposals. If health and social care practitioners find it difficult to separate 'need' from 'need for a specific service',[9,10] then desired outcomes that fall beyond the current limits of social care service provision risk remaining unmet.

1.3 What outcomes do older people value?

Qureshi et al[11] identified three clusters of social care outcomes valued by older people: change outcomes; maintenance or prevention outcomes; and process outcomes relating to the ways that services are delivered.

1.3.1 Change outcomes

'Change' outcomes relate to improvements in physical, mental or emotional functioning that are achieved through service interventions. Qureshi et al[11] found that older people value the following:

- changes in symptoms and behaviour; for example, older people with mental illness may wish to feel less anxious or depressed, to relate better to family members and to be more active and interested in life
- improvements in physical functioning, whether through improvements in individual mobility or through the provision of equipment and adaptations
- improving confidence and morale; older people anticipated feeling 'happier' if they received services that met their needs and addressed their problems.

1.3.2 Maintenance or prevention outcomes

The majority of the outcomes valued by older people relate to maintenance or preventing deterioration in their health, wellbeing or quality of life.

Meeting basic physical needs:

- being clean and presentable in appearance
- having appropriate food and drink at appropriate times
- being physically comfortable.[11–13]

Ensuring personal safety and security:

- Minimising fear of crime and threats to personal safety. Personal safety is particularly important for older people with dementia and can also be important in decisions to enter residential care. Feeling safe includes receiving services from people who can be 'vouched for' and trusted.[11, 13–15]

Living in a clean and tidy environment:

- An untidy house or garden is a threat to self-esteem as it can indicate that an older person is less able to manage her/his own affairs.
- A clean and comfortable home can help to sustain social inclusion, as older people are more likely to feel confident having visitors if the home is clean, tidy and continues to reflect their social identity.[15–17]
- However, it can be difficult to get social care support in this area and even when services are available, they may not be culturally appropriate[15, 16, p 11]. One group of minority ethnic older people opted for direct payments in order to obtain culturally appropriate home care services.[18]

Keeping alert and active:

- This includes preventing boredom and having activities that sustain competence, identity and independence. Losing a sense of purpose can be damaging to mental health. Remaining active also helps to sustain social interaction.[11, 17, 19–22]

- Keeping alert and active is particularly important to older people in residential settings; the range of activities available – including opportunities to pursue individual hobbies, undertake tasks related to the running of the home, excursions and outings – is an important dimension of the quality of homes as rated by older people[13, 23, 24, quoted in 25, p 13].

- Opportunities to go out and activities that result in a sense of achievement are also important for older people with dementia.[23]

Access to social contact and company:

- Close relationships and social networks are central to wellbeing in later life.
- For isolated older people, social contacts with home care staff are particularly valued.[17, 19, 22, 26, 27]
- Avoiding dependence on others is widely valued; consequently the benefits of social contact are enhanced if relationships are characterised by reciprocity. Accepting practical help and/or emotional support can be easier if there are opportunities to reciprocate[17, 21, 28, 29, 30 quoted in 25].
- Social contact is important for older people with dementia as it can promote a sense of continuing social integration.[14, 17, 23]
- Good quality social relationships – friendships with other residents and friendly staff attitudes – are important outcomes for older people in residential settings.[13, 31]

Having control over everyday life:

- This underpins all other outcomes relating to maintenance and prevention. Being 'looked after' involves a loss of control and therefore of independence; older people therefore want services that support them in looking after themselves. Having control over everyday life does not necessarily mean doing everything for oneself, but being able to decide how and when things are done.[5, 11, 12, 15, 17, 27, 29]
- Older people with dementia also value autonomy and control, including control over delegating some responsibilities to another person who they trust.[11, 14, 23]

- Choice and control over daily living activities are important outcomes for care home residents.[13, 31, 32]

1.3.3 Process outcomes

Process outcomes refer to users' experiences of seeking, obtaining and using services. Process outcomes are so important that they can undermine the impact of other outcomes that might otherwise improve quality of life. Barriers to process outcomes include lack of information; difficulties gaining access to services; delays in receiving services; inefficient or disrespectful staff; lack of consultation; and consultation that is not acted on.[11, 12, 16] The quality of relationships with staff and the personal attributes of the latter are crucial to positive outcomes and are valued equally by older people in their own homes and in residential care.[13, 16] Process outcomes include:

- Feeling valued and respected, despite cultural differences or communication difficulties; respect for privacy and confidentiality; and being treated as having a legitimate right to services. Feeling valued and respected is particularly important for older people with mental health problems or dementia.[12, 14, 33, 34]
- Being treated as an individual. Interpersonal aspects of service exchanges can assume great importance; older people want to feel at ease with social care staff and value willingness, responsiveness, cheerfulness, friendliness, understanding and an instinctive caring nature. Such attributes may be valued as highly as practical help and rated more highly than formal professional qualifications.[15, 29, 34–36]
- 'Having a say' and control over services, including the tasks and timing of services and who delivers them. Punctuality is important for some older people, particularly those with special medical needs.[14, 26, 34, 36] Having control includes being able to make a contribution – being an active participant rather than a passive recipient.[15, 19] This is important for people in residential care settings, who may value being able to contribute to preparing meals, for example.[12] 'Having a say' requires information, opportunities to discuss possible options with a knowledgeable person and being informed about changes in services. Older people from minority ethnic groups may require providers who

can speak their own language in order to 'have a say'.[11, 34] 'Having a say' also requires services to be flexible in response to changes in older people's capacities and preferences – this is particularly important for those living alone.[7, 15, 22, 26, 34]

- Value for money, whether services are privately purchased or users contribute means-tested co-payments.[11]
- A good 'fit' with informal sources of support, especially if services prevent unwanted reliance on family care.[11, 15]
- Compatibility with, and respect for, cultural and religious preferences.[34]

Table 1
Summary of social care outcomes desired by older people

Outcomes involving change
Changes in symptoms and behaviour
Improvements in physical functioning
Improving morale
Outcomes involving maintenance or prevention
Meeting basic physical needs
Ensuring personal safety and security
Living in a clean and tidy environment
Keeping alert and active
Access to social contact and company
Having control over everyday life
Service process outcomes
Feeling valued and being treated with respect
Being treated as an individual
Having 'a say' and control over services
Value for money
A 'good fit' with informal sources of support
Compatibility with, and respect for, cultural and religious preferences

1.3.4 Outcomes and diversity

Wealth, health status, gender, living arrangements and ethnicity all contribute to the diversity of older people's attitudes and aspirations[37]. The previous sections have highlighted outcomes that are particularly important to older people with dementia, from black and minority ethnic communities, and living in residential care. In general, different groups of older people prioritise different outcomes and dimensions of quality of life[8, 27, p 760].

Netten et al[38] found that people aged 85+ were more concerned about food and nutritional outcomes and less concerned about social contact than younger respondents; people living with others ranked social participation and involvement much higher than those living alone. Older people with recent sight loss also prioritise different outcomes,[39] as follows:

- meeting people and friendship
- getting information and advice about specialist services and equipment
- having someone to talk to about personal feelings
- building confidence to go out and do things outside the home
- relearning how to carry out everyday tasks in the home
- getting help with practical everyday tasks.

There is relatively little evidence on the specific outcomes desired by minority ethnic elders; much of the research literature focuses on barriers to care. However, despite their diversity, maintaining independence and having cultural needs recognised are commonly desired outcomes. Askham et al[40] found that specific language and food provision was important to many black older people, although for Afro-Caribbean elders being treated fairly, kindly and efficiently was more important.

Reviews by Mold et al[41] of Asian and other minority ethnic older people in care homes and by Butt and Mirza of black communities and social care[42] provide examples of how older people from minority ethnic groups value the process outcome of compatibility with, and respect for, individual cultural and other preferences, including:

- sensitivity to religious beliefs and practices
- interpreting services
- staff from similar backgrounds
- same-sex workers for intimate personal care
- halal and vegetarian food
- opportunities to meet others from similar backgrounds.

Older people with dementia particularly value efforts to ensure that they can communicate preferences; maximise control over daily life;[43] and keep alert and stimulated.[44] Culturally appropriate services, methods of working, language and communication (including non-verbal communication) were also highlighted in a study of minority ethnic older people with dementia (although information was obtained from professionals rather than older people themselves).[44]

1.3.5   Views of the User Advisory Group

Members of the User Advisory Group endorsed the importance of the outcomes identified in research with older people, particularly the recognition of individual needs and differences. However, they pointed out that some older people might need help to think about the outcomes they want from someone who knows their situation 'in the round'. These outcomes may not necessarily be what other people, such as carers, consider is 'best' for them – negotiation and trade-offs are necessary. There was strong agreement about the critical importance of choice and control; transport was also essential so that older people could take advantage of available services.

1.4 Organisational arrangements impeding outcomes-focused services

1.4.1   Introduction

This section draws particularly on research into the organisation and impact of home care services. Since the 1993 community care reforms, policies have prioritised supporting older people in their own homes. This has led to a major expansion in home care services, especially for very frail older people who would otherwise risk entering institutional care. Recent research mirrors these policy developments.

The 1993 reforms encouraged quasi-markets, with local authority social services departments purchasing services from voluntary and for-profit providers. Much recent research therefore focuses on the operation of quasi-markets in delivering outcomes-focused services. More recent developments in social services assessment, care planning and commissioning following initiatives such as Fair Access to Care Services (FACS) guidance and the Single Assessment Process (SAP) are not yet reflected in published research.

1.4.2 Assessment

Assessments are important in establishing eligibility for services and can establish a baseline of desired outcomes against which later achievements can be checked.[35] Outcomes-focused approaches can be inhibited by bureaucratic approaches in which practitioners report spending less time with users and increasingly routinised procedures [45, quoted in (19, p 11) 46]. Outcomes-focused approaches are not encouraged by service-led rather than needs-led assessments.[11, 47] Desired outcomes may be ignored because of health and safety concerns; thus lifting and handling restrictions can reduce older people's movement and create unnecessary dependence [19, p 21].

The language used in assessments can be a barrier to an outcomes-focused approach. Assessments need to be compatible with older people's identity and self-image otherwise potential service use may be discouraged.[48] Thus older people who define themselves as competent will refuse services that emphasise their dependency.[19]

Despite policies to the contrary, in practice assessments can overlook emotional and psychological needs and the meanings older people attach to these.[19, 49, 50] It is possible that recent 'assessment approaches vary markedly across local authorities and are likely to be less responsive to certain needs of older people (for example, depression)' [25, p 39]. Indeed, one study found that developments in practice following the NSF for older people and FACS have indeed reduced the risk of assessment overlooking older people's emotional and psychological needs; however, no research evidence was found on the impact of these measures.

Older people's services remain under-funded.[51] Thus staff conducting assessments may find themselves juggling conflicting roles of 'neutral facilitator', 'impartial advisor' and resource 'gate-keeper'. Hardy et al [52, p 487] found that 'strict financial controls and cost-ceilings constituted major constraints on [care managers'] ability to operate within and between these roles'. These resource constraints may lead to some desired outcomes being overlooked.

Older people themselves may find outcomes-focused assessments difficult, with their ability to identify outcomes restricted by their perceptions of social services' responsibilities; of the help they think it legitimate to request; and of the services they think are available.[19] Older people from minority ethnic groups are particularly disadvantaged in knowing what services are available[42] and in any case may not use services if they are perceived as culturally inappropriate.[53]

Being able to make choices about services is crucial to the outcomes of having control over everyday life and having a say. However, Hardy et al[52] found that during assessments older people and carers were offered little choice between services or how these were provided. For some users, choices may be restricted by a shortage of providers, a particular problem in rural areas,[9] or where purchasers contract only with lowest cost providers.

1.4.3   Reviews

Outcomes-focused approaches are facilitated by regular reviews that monitor service quality and ensure services continue to meet the outcomes identified at assessment or that reflect changed circumstances. However, this is difficult if, as sometimes happens, assessment and review activities are organisationally fragmented or conducted by different staff.[9]

Moreover, workload pressures on social services staff may mean that reviews are conducted irregularly, if at all.[34, 35, 54] Domiciliary Care Standards Regulations (2003) require all providers to review their customers at least annually, but this may be unduly onerous for providers with high numbers of users receiving only small levels of services.[26] Hardy et al [52, p 489] also found review procedures to be underdeveloped and variable, both within and between social services authorities. Formal reviews and re-assessments occurred for only 42 per cent of social services clients during 2001–2002.[55] Reviews are likely to concentrate on older people whose services are provided by independent agencies rather than in-house providers, on new service users and on users considered problematic.[26, 52]

Although some social services authorities have established special review teams, these disrupt the continuity of relationships between users and care managers. Fragmentation may be further encouraged by performance indicators that measure user and carer assessments, reviews and satisfaction surveys as separate activities.

1.4.4 Purchasing of care 'packages'

How care managers 'purchase' services from providers can create barriers to outcomes-focused services. Again it is important to note that the research reviewed here was conducted before the publication of FACS guidance; no research was found that evaluates the impact of this guidance on care managers' purchasing activities.

The 1980s community care demonstration projects gave care managers small caseloads and devolved budgets to purchase flexible, individually tailored services.[46, 56] However, since 1993 care managers have had less face-to-face contact with clients; adopted increasingly routinised approaches; and been restricted by financial constraints.[9, 46] There are significant variations between social services departments in their care management arrangements[46, p 682], particularly whether the services commissioned extend beyond basic physical maintenance to wider, quality of life outcomes.[57] There are also variations in the autonomy devolved by care managers to front-line service providers,[26, 46, 57] with some provider managers frustrated by inflexible and uncompromising commissioning arrangements. For example, if no allowance is made for time spent travelling between appointments, home care staff may be tempted (or encouraged by their manager) to curtail visits once essential tasks are completed. Changes that users wish to make to the content or timing of a service may have to be notified to care managers and new assessments conducted.[26, 34, 36] Such restrictions may be particularly true of services commissioned from independent (voluntary and for-profit), rather than in-house, providers.[57]

Purchasing home care services for specified periods of time or for specific tasks has different implications for services' ability to meet desired outcomes:[26]

- 'Time-centred' visits are easier to deliver punctually.
- The costs of 'time-centred' visits are easier to calculate, which may affect user perceptions of value for money.
- 'Time-centred' visits offer opportunities to undertake extra tasks or just talk once essential jobs are completed.
- 'Task-centred' visits can be extended or shortened according to changing circumstances.

Barriers to outcomes-focused home care services arise when social services purchasers place restrictions on the range of tasks they are willing to pay for. Older people have expressed particular concern about the lack of help with housework and other domestic tasks,[9, 15, 34] despite the fact that having a clean and orderly home environment is an important maintenance outcome.[15]

A further barrier is the failure by care managers to recognise the importance of relationships between older people and paid care staff; the quality of these is central to process outcomes. Thus older people may benefit from any spare time left in 'time-centred' visits if care staff can use this simply to talk. However, some care managers discourage the development of such relationships as 'unprofessional'.[15, 26]

1.4.5 Provider-level barriers

The environment within which independent (voluntary and for-profit) service providers operate can also impact on the delivery of outcomes-focused services. Relationships with staff are crucially important to the process outcomes of social care. However, these relationships can be impaired by poor continuity, which can itself be impaired by problems of recruiting and retaining staff.[9, 47, 56]

There are substantial shortfalls in provider capacity, including both numbers of organisations (particularly in rural areas) and problems of staff recruitment and retention (particularly in rural, affluent and inner-city areas). Since 1993, both overall demand for home care services and the range and complexity of skills required of staff have increased, while the shift from in-house to independent sector provision may have worsened pay and conditions for some staff. These factors affect staff recruitment and retention; their availability to work the hours that users prefer;[9, 22, 26, 47] and ultimately the reliability, quality and responsiveness of services.[26] For example, feeling in control of daily life requires the delivery of services at times that fit in with daily routines.[11] This can be jeopardised if providers cannot meet heavy demand early in the mornings and in the evenings.[22]

The organisational arrangements of provider organisations also affect relationship-based process outcomes. Relevant arrangements include the basis on which home care staff are employed (part-time, full-time, guaranteed pay per week or pay per case and so on); the number of workers allocated to each older person; and organisations' policies on requests for additional or different tasks to be performed from those set out in the care plan.[26] For example, some providers prohibit staff from carrying out tasks such as changing light bulbs, finding a plumber or caring for pets that are unproblematic in other organisations.[57]

Independent providers whose business depends on a few large local authority block contracts may be unwilling to respond to older people's requests for additional privately purchased help to meet desired outcomes because of anxieties about jeopardising their main contracts.[26, 57] Providers may also be reluctant to offer low-skilled domestic help like shopping and housecleaning for private purchase by older people; having invested in staff training, providers may be reluctant to ask staff to do lower-skilled work. Patmore[26] found providers anxious about being typecast as low skilled – and therefore low cost. This assumption could be at odds with the actual costs of delivering a quality service and disadvantage providers in Best Value reviews.

1.4.6   Role of commissioners

Commissioners exert major influences over whether providers deliver outcomes-focused services.[26, 57, 58] There is some evidence[26, 57] that these influences are particularly marked in relation to independent sector, rather than in-house, services.

One strand of research has examined how commissioning arrangements affect providers' motivation. Some providers reported poor relationships with commissioners, complaining of late payments; poor review and follow-up of clients; low prices; and systematic biases towards in-house providers. Any poor performance by providers was related to this dissatisfaction.[52, 59-61] Some in-house service managers reported that the purchaser/provider split had made them subordinate to people they previously regarded as their social worker peers and this was demoralising.[26]

Different types of contract (spot, block, call-off, cost-and-volume and grants) can affect the responsiveness and quality of home care.[58] Some local authorities operate 'cheapest first' policies when setting contracts for home care services;[9] driving down costs can drive down quality. The contracts for home care services offered by many authorities have been criticised for being short term and including conditions that may be unattractive to providers.[59]

Many contracts contain little flexibility to vary prices. This helps purchasers plan their expenditure (and may also help safeguard provider stability), but makes providers vulnerable to risk arising from changes in costs that occur during a contract and reduces their ability to tailor services to individual users' requests and circumstances. Flexible, spot-purchasing or contingency-sensitive pricing would shift some of the risk back to purchasers and provide greater incentives to providers to respond to changes in users' circumstances.[59]

1.4.7 Importance of communication

Research emphasises the importance of communication between providers and purchasers for outcomes-focused services. Communication is important:

- Between care managers, commissioners and providers, '… if contracts with providers are to be adjusted to reflect user need and preference'[9, p 418].
- Between providers and care managers, with the latter communicating service users' preferred outcomes; and providers keeping care managers informed about changes in their policies and practices and in users' circumstances.[9]
- Between provider managers and front-line home care staff, so that changes in circumstances or requests for different types of help are quickly identified.

- Between users, providers and purchasers, with clarity over who is responsible for notifying users of changes in services.
- Between front-line staff, if more than one worker is involved with an older person.

Barriers to communication at any of these points can threaten the flexibility and responsiveness of home care services.[34]

Care managers and front-line staff also have significant roles to play in providing older people with the information they may need to achieve desired outcomes. However, social care services often lack the resources to develop, maintain and regularly update their information databases, particularly about services, benefits and facilities outside the remit of their own agency, thereby restricting staff capacity to fulfil this role.[47]

1.4.8 Impact of the health–social care divide

The division between health and social care responsibilities can be a barrier to outcomes-focused services and a source of frustration to service users.[62] Godfrey and Callaghan [19, p 5] found that '... health and social care needs were inextricably tied in with [older] people's social and emotional lives ... need could not be categorised as "social" or "medical"'.

However, social services care managers may be unaware of the potential for change outcomes that could result from improvements in functional abilities; health professionals may fail to appreciate that some disabilities can be improved by a range of non-health services.[63] There is also considerable under-identification of mental health problems among older people, including those receiving social services,[64, 65] despite evidence of the interrelationship between mental health, physical disability and poor social networks. A combination of services, including both medical treatment and social support, is therefore likely to be appropriate in maximising change outcomes.[66]

Ware et al [9, p 420] found that separate budgets for health and social care undermined joint working. The SAP, partnerships using Section 31 of the Health Act 1999 and collaborative working in response to the introduction of reimbursement for delayed discharges may all have contributed to reducing the operational barriers between health and social care services for older people. However, no research into the impact of these initiatives on the delivery of outcomes-focused services has yet been published.

1.4.9 Barriers and diversity

Research into the experiences of minority ethnic older people focuses more on barriers to accessing services than outcomes. Barriers to receiving good quality care include lack of knowledge about services; language and communication barriers; and scepticism about the appropriateness and cultural sensitivity of services.[41, 42, 67] In some localities there may be few specialised services, particularly in residential settings, although day centres and lunch clubs are more common.[40] Research with professionals into provision for minority ethnic older people with dementia has also identified culturally inappropriate services, as well as lack of resources and poor coordination between services.[44]

1.4.10 Views of the User Advisory Group

Members of the User Advisory Group endorsed these findings. They confirmed that assessment processes could be too bureaucratic; and that there are many tasks important to older people that social care services do not help with, such as cleaning, gardening and taking clients out shopping (rather than doing their shopping for them). The quality of home care services was thought to be affected by the low pay and low status of many staff, which leads to high staff turnover. In addition, the privatisation of many care services was thought to have increased communication problems, particularly between staff carrying out assessments and front-line care staff – for this reason in-house services were perceived to be more reliable. The charges that users pay for home care services were perceived as expensive, potentially restricting some people from using services and achieving desired outcomes.

1.5 Organisational arrangements facilitating outcomes-focused services

1.5.1 Introduction

This section focuses on evidence about the organisational arrangements that can promote outcomes-focused services. In particular, it highlights several projects conducted by the Social Policy Research Unit (SPRU) at the University of York that developed and tested with local authority partners ways that social care services could collect and use information about the outcomes valued by users, as part of routine practice. These projects were evaluated to assess their feasibility and impact. Other evidence is derived from broader research projects investigating the delivery of social care services; this evidence sometimes includes recommendations that have not been subject to thorough evaluation.

1.5.2 Assessment

While assessments may identify activities with which help is needed, they may fail to specify the ways in which older people wish help to be given, including practices consistent with personal, cultural or religious preferences. Outcomes-focused assessments therefore need to include these issues and incorporate them into the care plans that are agreed with service providers.[34, 36]

Qureshi[68] developed documentation to summarise outcomes and preferences when older people are assessed. The documents aimed to link identified needs to service delivery by giving clear information to providers about what they were expected to achieve. The documentation recorded desired change and maintenance outcomes and preferences relating to process outcomes. Documentation included:

- summary of needs
- expected changes that could affect future service delivery
- a summary of agreed outcomes
- options and preferences for achieving these outcomes.

Feedback on the documentation was obtained from social workers/care managers; this was generally positive. Negative comments concerned the complexity and unfamiliarity of outcomes-focused approaches and the time required to complete the assessment, although this was expected to reduce with practice. Staff agreed that explicit recording of desired outcomes could:

- differentiate more clearly between good and less good practice
- clarify the basis for care plan decisions; improve the skills of care managers; help to focus services; and provide the basis for subsequent reviews
- contribute to computerised client information systems.

Potential implementation barriers included:

- staff reluctance to adopt new documentation and assessment procedures
- staff uncertainty about outcomes and their application to social care practice
- workload and other organisational pressures.

1.5.3 Reviews

Conceiving of review as a continuous process rather than a discrete event may ensure desired outcomes continue to be achieved.[9] Other ways of ensuring services remain compatible with desired outcomes include audits of service users; focus groups with purchasers and providers; quality assurance schemes informed by users; user-led interviews; and diaries kept by service users.[22, 69, 70] However, none of these has been evaluated.

Nicholas[71, 72] developed and tested tools to improve assessments and reviews of carers; similar tools could be adapted for older people. The tools aimed to:

- involve carers in identifying needs and desired outcomes during assessment
- vary assessment approaches according to individual circumstances and preferences
- facilitate discussion about and recording of intended service outcomes

- provide a framework for aggregating outcomes information to inform service developments.

Evaluation of the project involved social services staff and carers themselves. It concluded that:

- carers felt recognised and 'listened to'
- staff valued their greater understanding of carers' needs and desired outcomes
- professional judgement and flexibility were essential in determining for whom, when and how the tools could be used most effectively
- limited resources and workload pressures could jeopardise the identification and monitoring of outcomes and reduce the usefulness of aggregate information.

The benefits of the tools were enhanced by involving carers in their development; by active management support; and by an enabling culture. It is not clear how far these instruments are compatible with current policy and practice following FACS and the SAP.

A further method of reviewing outcomes involved using postal questionnaires[73] to collect information on the outcomes of occupational therapy assessments and the subsequent provision of equipment and adaptations. Users, carers and staff and managers were involved in designing:

- questionnaires about minor adaptations or equipment and major adaptations
- a questionnaire for carers

Questions about quality of life and service process outcomes were included. Good response rates were achieved (including responses from people aged over 80) through the use of reminders.

The project concluded that this approach was generalisable to other services, depending on the characteristics of service users, the types and diversity of outcomes and the extent to which an outcomes focus was consistent with the values and routine practice of staff. Again, the feasibility of this approach was enhanced by commitment from managers and by front-line staff having a clear understanding of outcomes. Appropriate management information systems were also important to success.

1.5.4 Micro-level commissioning of care 'packages'

Francis and Netten[34] argue that care managers' roles should be restricted to assessing needs and allocating resources, with providers having autonomy to agree with users exactly how those resources are used. Patmore[26] recommended that care managers should purchase a monthly allowance of unallocated time to be used by front-line home care staff as circumstances require. However, there is no evidence on the effectiveness of such approaches, nor on whether different care management arrangements are more or less efficient and effective in delivering outcomes-focused services.[46, 59]

One approach to micro-level commissioning that has been demonstrated to have benefits, at least for some older people, is to devolve responsibility for micro-purchasing to older people themselves by substituting direct payments for services in kind. Because direct payments offer increased choice and control, they have significant potential to enable older people to achieve desired outcomes. However, take-up of direct payments by older people has been much less extensive than by younger disabled people and research evidence is similarly limited. The one available study[18, 74] shows that older people were able to achieve considerably more of the outcomes they valued, particularly support to get out and go shopping; help with tasks within the home that conventional home care services were unable to perform; and improvements in personal safety and health. However, achieving these outcomes depended on local support services that were inclusive of older people.

1.5.5 Provider-level factors

Initiatives that have been suggested to improve the recruitment and retention of home care staff, and therefore enhance process outcomes for older people, include: premium payments for unsocial working hours or inconvenient locations; bonus rates for extra work in response to occasional requests from users; mileage allowances for travel between customers; and guaranteeing staff a specific amount of work each week. Patmore[26] argues for a mix of incentives and bonus payments, depending on the particular staffing difficulties experienced by a provider, in order to retain experienced staff and meet users' requests for services at specific times and places. None of these suggestions has been evaluated to assess the impact on the outcomes orientation of home care services.

1.5.6   Importance of communication

The previous sections have noted a number of points in the operation of quasi-markets in which clear communication is essential in achieving outcomes-focused services. Measures that have been shown to help includes extensive feedback between purchasers and providers; enabling providers to feel in control of their services; and creating communication channels that recognise provider expertise.[61]

One initiative to improve communication between staff carrying out assessments and front-line service providers involved an outcomes-focused briefing sheet for home care staff. This ensured that individual preferences, priorities and desired process outcomes were routinely identified and communicated by care managers to front-line home care staff.[75] Evaluation showed that the briefing sheet was useful in enabling desired outcomes to be pursued more consistently and in delivering more individualised services. It also reminded home care staff to undertake rehabilitation or 'enablement' activities with older people, identify new needs, or persuade reluctant users to accept extra services.

1.5.7   Overcoming the health–social care divide

Research on the implementation of the Health Act flexibilities[76] focused on their organisational, financial and governance consequences. Indeed, much research on health and social care partnerships has focused on process issues rather than user outcomes.[77] Research is currently (2006) in progress into the outcomes that older people and other groups of service users expect from health and social care partnerships. Interim findings from this research indicate these outcomes mirror closely those identified in the first part of this review, but with a particular emphasis on process and maintenance outcomes.[78] Another study, also in progress, is investigating the impact of the Health Act flexibilities on the delivery of positive outcomes for frail and vulnerable older people. Interim findings reveal that the main service area in which the flexibilities are being used is intermediate care.[78]

1.5.8 Initiatives and diversity

Individualised approaches to communication and consultation can help people with dementia to articulate their views and preferences. Maximising their control over opportunities for communication, using pictures, using the older person's own vocabulary and phrasing and interpreting non-verbal communication can be effective, although they require time and confidence on the part of staff.[43] Specialist services and staff with skills in communicating with people with little language are vital to maintain quality of life of people with dementia in residential settings.[79] Recommendations from a Health Action Zone project for improving outcomes for minority ethnic elders with dementia include involving professionals from outside the locality to maintain confidentiality; and working in partnership with religious communities.[80] Again these initiatives focus more generally on improving access to services rather than achieving desired outcomes.

1.5.9 Views of the User Advisory Group

Members of the User Advisory Group called for better training, pay and status for front-line home care staff. They also pointed to the potential role of GPs in helping to overcome the health–social care divide; GPs are in regular contact with many older people and can help them to access social services. It was thought that the new community matrons might also be able to fulfil this role.

However, members of the group also drew attention to the problems some older people have in accessing or accepting social care services. They pointed out that some older people find the name off-putting; older people from minority ethnic communities may have to overcome language barriers, a particular difficulty if children have been born in England and do not speak the community language and so cannot interpret for their parents. Social services could address this problem of access by developing closer links with voluntary organisations such as Age Concern, who are likely to be more easily accessible to many older people. Adequate funding for these organisations is essential.

1.6 Conclusions of research review

Outcomes widely desired by older people relate to change, maintenance or prevention and the processes of receiving services. These are congruent with the dimensions of wellbeing and independence, as defined by older people. However, research shows that barriers relating to the operation of quasi-markets can impede the achievement of outcomes. Additional barriers for minority ethnic elders arise from a shortage of culturally appropriate services.

Initiatives to improve outcomes-focused services have involved improving communication between users, front-line providers, care managers and purchasers. However, evaluation of these has tended to focus on their implementation; there is still a lack of evidence on the effectiveness of initiatives in improving user outcomes.

Practice survey

2.1 Introduction to practice survey

This practice survey complements a review of published research into the outcomes of social care services desired by older people and the factors that inhibit or contribute to the implementation of outcomes-focused approaches.

The practice survey aimed to:

- identify features of the social care policy and practice environments that support or inhibit the development of outcomes-focused approaches in older people's services
- identify examples of outcomes-focused organisational arrangements and approaches that provide opportunities for wider learning
- explore how localities intend to build on existing practice to implement proposals in the Green Paper on adult social care.[2]
- explore older people's perspectives on the impact of outcomes-focused approaches.

The practice survey had two parts:

- a postal survey of social care staff in England and Wales known to be interested in developing outcomes-focused approaches in older people's services
- in-depth studies of services in six localities currently using outcomes-focused approaches in their service commissioning and/or delivery.

The methods used in the practice survey are described in Appendix 2. Details of the outcomes-focused activities and services in the six case study sites are contained in Appendix 3.

Details of some other local outcomes-based initiatives were obtained directly from members of the Outcomes Network that was set up as part of the Department of Health-funded Outcomes of Social Care Research and Development Programme conducted by the Social Policy Research Unit at the University of York between 2000 and 2005. The Network is now called the Better Commissioning Learning and Information Network (LIN) and is part of the Department of Health Change Agent Team (www.changeagentteam.org.uk/better_commiss).

The two-stage design – postal survey and in-depth case studies – means that the practice survey had both breadth and depth. SPRU's Outcomes Network brought together a relatively small number of managers who were keen to develop outcomes-focused approaches in their localities. The Network therefore provided opportunities to test out new approaches and learn from the experiences of others. However, members of the Network were self-selecting and thus may not be representative. Moreover, the support derived from the Network was not typical of the environment in which managers in other localities may try to introduce outcomes-focused changes to their older people's services. With an explicit policy focus on outcomes in the adult social care Green Paper[2] and the UK strategy for an ageing population,[3] it was important to capture the wider environment in which social services managers are now attempting to introduce outcomes-focused services. The postal survey therefore aimed to identify the range of initiatives across England and Wales and to capture wide-ranging views on the main facilitating factors and obstacles.

However, postal surveys have limitations, particularly in capturing information likely to be useful in replicating outcomes-focused initiatives, or the different perspectives of stakeholders such as managers, front-line staff and service users. The six case studies, involving interviews and discussions with managers, front-line staff and service users, therefore provided a more detailed account of local activities.

A User Advisory Group was established to guide the knowledge review (*see* Appendix 1).

2.2 Postal survey

2.2.1 Aims

The aims of the postal survey were:

- to ascertain the range and nature of outcomes-focused initiatives being developed by social care services (and partner organisations) for older people
- to identify factors considered to facilitate or hinder outcomes-focused approaches in social care
- to identify a small number of localities for in-depth investigation.

2.2.2 Methods

The postal survey was targeted at individuals and organisations known to have an interest in outcomes-focused social care services. An extensive list of relevant contacts had been developed by SPRU; many of these are now members of the Better Commissioning Learning and Information Network. However, some contacts were out of date; others were of people working with disabled adults or children. An extensive updating and screening exercise was therefore conducted (*see* Appendix 2), so that the postal survey could be targeted at a specific group – people in England and Wales who were known actually to have developed or be interested in developing outcomes-focused approaches in older people's services. Full details of the survey methods are reported in Appendix 2.

2.2.3 Respondent characteristics

Two hundred and twenty-two questionnaires were sent out to individuals and organisations in England (*n*=200) and Wales (*n*=22). Following reminder letters and emails, 54 valid responses were received, including six from Wales. These covered at least 70 service developments (some respondents described an unspecified number of activities).

Most respondents (87 per cent) worked in local authorities/social services (*see* Table 2), including six who had joint appointments with another organisation. Nine organisations returned two (*n*=4) or three questionnaires (*n*=5), with different respondents describing their involvement in the same or different initiatives within these organisations; the total number of organisations is therefore less than the total number of respondents. This report refers to the number of respondents rather than organisations or areas.

Table 2
Organisations in which respondents worked*

Organisation	Number of respondents
Local authority/social services	47
NHS acute trust	3
Voluntary organisation	3
Primary care trust	2
Private consulting	2
Other (includes local health boards; NHS care trust; Change Agent Team)	4

Note: * Some respondents worked in two or more organisations, hence the total number exceeds the number of respondents (n=54).

Thirty-six respondents (67 per cent) reported on outcomes-focused services involving two or more organisations, including 22 involving primary care trusts and 18 involving NHS trusts (see Table 3). Twenty-one respondents reported working with independent providers on outcomes-focused services. In cases of joint working, 46 per cent of respondents (n=25) identified local authorities/social services as the lead agency.

2.2.4 Nature and range of outcomes work

Many of the 70 initiatives that respondents described were at early stages of development (see Table 4). Only seven respondents described initiatives that had been established for three years or longer. All six Welsh respondents were involved in initiatives that were still at the planning stage.

Respondents were engaged in a wide range of outcomes-focused activities, with 'planning services that aim to identify and achieve outcomes valued by older people' the most common (see Table 5). The seven projects that had been established for three years or more were more likely to be described as 'involving older people in the design and development of outcomes-focused services' and 'promoting outcomes-

Table 3
Respondents whose outcomes work involved other organisations*

Other organisations involved in outcomes-focused work	Number of respondents
Primary care trust	22
Private service provider	21
Local authority/social services	20
NHS acute trust	18
Voluntary organisation	18
Private consultancy	5
Other organisations (housing/registered social landlords, local health boards, service user forums)	7

Note: * Respondents' outcomes work may have involved more than one type of organisation.

Table 4
Stages of outcomes-focused projects

Stage	Number of projects reported by respondents*	% sample $n=54$
Established 3 years or more	7	13
Established 3 years or less	9	17
Currently being 'rolled out'	18	33
Currently being piloted	12	22
In planning stages	21	39
Other stage	2	4
n/a	1	2

Note: * Some respondents were involved in more than one project and reported the different stages of development of each.

Table 5
Types of outcomes-focused service developments

Type of work	Number of respondents	% sample n=54
Planning changes to identify and achieve valued outcomes	44	81
Monitoring/evaluating the effectiveness of outcomes-focused services	35	65
Commissioning services to identify and achieve valued outcomes	31	57
Providing services to identify and achieve valued outcomes	26	48
Involving older people in the development of outcomes-focused services	26	48
Outcomes-focused approaches to supporting carers of older people	21	39
Other types of outcomes-focused services	9	17
Independent consultancy/ development work with social care services	6	11

focused approaches to supporting carers of older people' than the sample as a whole.

Outcomes-focused initiatives most often involved services for older people living at home and least often services for older people in residential care (*see* Table 6). However, five of the seven longest-established initiatives (three years plus) also included older people in residential care.

Table 6
Groups of older people covered by outcomes initiatives

Group	Number of respondents	% sample n=54
Older people living at home	50	93
Older people immediately after discharge from hospital	48	89
Older people with dementia	44	81
Older people from black and minority ethnic groups	42	78
Carers of older people	41	76
Older people in day care	41	76
Older people in hospital prior to discharge	41	76
Older people in residential care	30	56

The specific activities that comprised the reported outcomes-focused work were diverse (*see* Table 7). The most frequent activities involved adapting assessment, care planning and reviews to focus on user outcomes. Most respondents who were engaged in these activities reported that they covered all older service users, but some reported their activities covered only 'some' rather than 'all' older people. Fourteen respondents reported being involved in all six areas of work for 'all' or 'some' groups of older people; these included five of the seven respondents reporting initiatives that had been established for three years plus. Respondents describing longer-established initiatives were also more likely to be involved in outcomes-focused service monitoring and evaluation than respondents as a whole.

The postal survey asked how far older people themselves had been involved in planning outcomes-focused developments (*see* Table 8). Only two of the seven respondents describing initiatives that had been established for three years or more reported involving older people 'greatly'.

Table 7
Focus of outcomes work

Focus of work	Number of respondents (n=for 'all' older people/ n=for 'some' older people)
Focus on outcomes in care planning	35 (27/8)
Identifying outcomes desired by individual older people at assessment	34 (24/10)
Reviewing whether outcomes desired by individual older people at assessment are achieved	33 (20/13)
Changing existing services to better meet older people's needs and preferences	26 (12/14)
Monitoring/evaluating services to examine the extent to which services meet desired outcomes	25 (11/14)
Commissioning/developing new services to better meet older people's needs and preferences	22 (10/12)

Table 8
Involvement of older people in planning outcomes work

Level of involvement	Number of respondents	% sample n=53
Greatly	6	11
Moderately	17	32
A little	19	36
Not at all	7	13
Don't know	3	6
No response	1	2

2.2.5 Achievements and factors helping and hindering achievements

Respondents were asked to identify the main achievements of their outcomes-focused work to date; the researchers coded their answers. A fifth of respondents did not complete this question, some of whom commented that it was 'too early to say'. Significantly, perceived achievements were as likely to relate to the effects on services as to the impact on service users (*see* Table 9).

Respondents identified a range of factors that helped and hindered progress in developing outcomes-focused services for older people; many also cited measures taken to overcome perceived barriers (*see* Table 10).

Of the 41 respondents who identified measures to overcome barriers, the majority (*n*=30) felt that these had been 'partly' or 'fully' successful, while the remainder thought it was 'too early to say'.

Table 9
Perceived achievements of outcomes work to date

Improvements in services	Effects on older people/carers
Modernisation of services	New or better quality services
Service ratings	for older people and their
Improved skills/engagement of	carers
staff	Better focus on individual
Service monitoring	needs and desired outcomes
Joint working	More person-centred/less
Decreased bureaucracy	service-led/more holistic
Changes in levels of service	approaches
provision	Empowerment of older people
Better use of resources	
Development of service	
specifications	

Table 10
Summary of factors that helped and hindered progress, and measures taken to overcome any perceived barriers

Factors	Examples of what has helped progress	Examples of what has hindered progress	Measures taken to overcome barriers
Training	External, in-house and joint training for health and social care staff; SPRU Outcomes training resources	Lack of training; arranging training for large numbers of staff	Developing training programmes/briefings; seconding staff
Joint working/ partnerships	Whole systems working with NHS/voluntary sector/ providers/older people forums; multidisciplinary teams; developing shared values and trust	Poor/immature partnerships; poor relationships with providers	Joint workshops; strategic partnerships; on-going work with providers

Factors	Examples of what has helped progress	Examples of what has hindered progress	Measures taken to overcome barriers
Staff attitudes, priorities	Commitment, enthusiasm, attitudes of staff at all levels to outcomes-focused approaches and related issues	Lack of commitment from key colleagues (managers, Chief Executive, IT department); partner agencies; providers Staff lack of understanding of outcomes Priority of performance measures/indicators Staff anxiety/resistance to change	Senior management leadership Regular discussions of outcomes focus
Organisational culture change	Organisational re-structuring to improve customer focus	Difficulties in initiating and sustaining changes in organisational culture	'Mainstreaming' outcomes approaches and user/carer involvement Using other changes to introduce outcomes approaches

Factors	Examples of what has helped progress	Examples of what has hindered progress	Measures taken to overcome barriers
Resources	Having sufficient resources to review and develop services; changing how resources are used	Funding pressures/limitations; financial assessment procedures; staff recruitment/retention	Using small projects to demonstrate change; more creative use of short-term and project funding to introduce new approaches/training
Recording systems/tools	New documentation that includes outcomes	Lack of IT capacity/flexibility; difficulties with new outcomes-focused paperwork	Changes in IT/data collection/monitoring/audit; new performance and workload management tools

Factors	Examples of what has helped progress	Examples of what has hindered progress	Measures taken to overcome barriers
External factors	Policy emphasis on: • independence and choice • UAP/SAP* • NSFs* for older people/long-term conditions • direct payments CSCI* outcomes-focused inspections Change Agent Team	Managing: • multiple policy priorities (FACS, SAP/UAP, charging, CSCI, NSFs, ESCR,* prevention) • workload pressures • resources vs targets • creativity vs risk • tensions between outcomes for services, for users and for carers	Challenged CSCI Links to chronic disease management initiatives

Note: FACS: Fair Access to Care Services, SAP: Single Assessment Process, UAP: Unified Assessment Process:, CSCI: Commission for Social Care Inspection, NSFs: National Service Frameworks, ESCR: electronic social care record

2.2.6 Postal survey: discussion

The postal survey was sent to individuals known to be involved in developing outcomes-focused approaches to services for older people. Nevertheless, despite repeated reminders the response rate was low (24 per cent). It is possible that there are other examples that were not captured by the survey.

However, the responses received suggest that there may not be many other established practice examples. Only 10 per cent of the reported developments had been established for at least three years, and another 13 per cent for up to three years. Three quarters of the reported initiatives were therefore being 'rolled out', 'piloted' or 'planned'. If outcomes-focused approaches are mainly very recent, then it is possible that non-responses reflected a lack of positive, substantive progress.

Members of the User Advisory Group also queried how far the survey results were accurate. In a number of instances, more than one response was received from the same organisation, allowing accounts to be cross-checked. User Advisory Group members suggested that the poor response rate could reflect the low priority given to older people's services. They were particularly concerned about the relatively low involvement of older people in outcomes-focused service developments and about the low priority that appeared to be given to monitoring and evaluation.

Not surprisingly, the longest-established initiatives appeared to have made most progress in terms of the number and range of activities involved and the range of older people covered. Even so, only a minority of these long-established initiatives reported the extensive involvement of older people in planning and monitoring activities.

Outcomes-focused initiatives were more likely to be described as 'planning', 'monitoring and evaluating' or 'commissioning' services that 'aim to identify and achieve the outcomes valued by older people', and least likely to involve 'supporting carers' of older people. Initiatives covered a wide range of older people in different situations, the most common being older people living at home and the least common being older people in residential care.

Factors that helped develop outcomes-focused approaches included training, joint working, staff attitudes and values, changes in organisational culture, resources, and appropriate documents and tools. National policies, such as the adult social care Green Paper, SAP, NSFs for older people/people with long-term conditions, the promotion of direct payments and new CSCI inspection methodologies were all cited as facilitating outcomes-focused approaches. However, these factors could simultaneously hinder progress if they generated too many (competing) priorities.

In summary, the postal survey suggests that English and Welsh social services departments are still only beginning to develop outcomes-focused services for older people. This also limited the selection of sites for in-depth study to the few that had made some progress in developing outcomes approaches (*see* Appendix 2).

2.3 Case studies

2.3.1 Introduction

This section describes findings from in-depth studies of six English localities that had been developing outcomes-focused approaches in some or all of their services for up to three years, or longer. It describes outcomes-focused approaches to assessment, care planning and review; to strategic planning, commissioning and contracting; and to services most commonly used by older people – home care, day care, intermediate and rehabilitation services (*see* Table 11). This section also includes some material obtained from the Better Commissioning LIN.

Some of the case study sites were 'high performing' according to national performance indicators; others were relatively poorly performing local authorities and/or social services departments. Several of the sites had recently been successful in applying for Partnerships for Older People Projects (POPPs) to develop new ways of delivering preventive services in collaboration with NHS and other local partners.

This section does not reflect the full extent of the outcomes-focused service developments under way in each site. Initial discussions with senior managers revealed that it was common for progress with outcomes-focused approaches to be unevenly spread across a locality's services and/or activities. The fieldwork therefore focused on those areas where most progress had been made, as these offered the greatest opportunities for learning. Section 2.3.5 below presents evidence on the

Table 11
Case study sites

Site	Activity	Services
Bradford	Assessment, care planning and review	Day care
Cumbria County Council	Assessment and care planning; home care services contracts	Intermediate care
Dorset County Council	Developing, commissioning and managing services	Prevention; community-based rehabilitation; home care
London Borough of Hillingdon	Commissioning and developing preventive services	Home care; rehabilitation services
North Lincolnshire Council	Care management	Residential care; home care
Worcestershire County Council	Commissioning; care management; contract specifications for new preventive services	Rehabilitation and reablement

See Appendix 3 for further details of the case study sites.

benefits (and limitations) of these changes from the perspectives of older service users.

Members of the User Advisory Group commented in detail on the draft topic guides that were used during the case study site visits and made many changes to the wording to make this compatible with the experiences and concerns of older people. They requested that a number of additional questions were asked of service managers, including:

- Would you be happy if your mother was receiving this service?
- Are you working closely with voluntary organisations?

- How far do social services share information with other relevant services/departments?
- If an assessment identifies an outcome that cannot be met by social services, is a referral made to another statutory or voluntary organisation?

2.3.2 Outcomes-focused activities

2.3.2.1 Assessment and care planning

The impact of SPRU's Outcomes Research Programme was apparent in the assessment and care planning documents used in several localities. However, these sites all noted the difficulties of incorporating an outcomes focus into the SAP. Different solutions had been found:

- One site had drawn a clear distinction between assessment (understanding difficulties and needs); and care planning (focused on desired outcomes). Its care plan listed 10 quality of life (maintenance) outcome domains and four rehabilitation (change) outcome domains; social workers indicated against each whether the aim was improvement or maintenance.
- In a second site, outcomes had been introduced into the care plan; care managers first identified the outcome; then the type of support required to make it happen; finally they recorded the need in the SAP. This was described as 'doing it the other way round to what we used to do'.
- A third site had adapted the EasyCare version of the SAP contact assessment form. In the section 'Planning your care', assessors were asked to seek users' views on:
  > 'Outcomes we can support you in achieving'
  > 'How these outcomes might be achieved (your care options)'
  > 'Your preferred choices from these options'.
  >> The summary care plan, now part of the SAP contact assessment paperwork, had also retained an outcomes focus. Alongside detailing the help that had been arranged and who would provide it, assessors also completed a column headed 'By providing this support we hope you will be able to...'. However, some managers

were disappointed not to have been able to retain a more explicit outcomes focus.

- As part of its response to the postal survey, one social services department sent its Needs and Care Planning tool that was also used by other services such as community nursing and the older people's mental health team. The tool incorporated FACS bandings as well as needs, actions and outcomes. The department was keen to make this document widely available as a Freeware tool; it had been posted on the Centre for Policy on Ageing website (www.cpa.org.uk).
- Northumberland Care Trust had adapted its outcomes approach to reflect FACS eligibility criteria; these were also included in their Community Care Charter.

2.3.2.2 Review

Even though it may be difficult to incorporate outcomes into SAP documentation, desired outcomes can still form the basis for reviews. An example of an outcomes-focused Review Assessment Form from one site is shown below; reviewers were asked to indicate changes under the following headings:

Outcome domains – review assessment	
• Increased physical abilities	• Quality of life maintained
• Higher morale	• Changes in behaviour
• Essential physical needs met	• Improved mental health
• Safer environment	• Have finances in order
• Increased confidence or skills	• Cleaner environment
• More social contact	• Risk(s) reduced/remove

Staff in this site felt positive about the review process. 'The paperwork keeps you in the right direction – it's prompting you all the way through…. Of all the paperwork, the review form is the best because you can look at what has been achieved.' Staff also had flexibility over when first reviews were conducted – essential with older people recently discharged from hospital.

2.3.2.3 Commissioning

Sites had made changes to commissioning and contracting arrangements with both in-house and independent providers to encourage more flexible, person-centred and outcomes-oriented services.

Commissioning for change outcomes – in-house services

Reflecting national policy initiatives relating to hospital admission and discharge, all case study sites had recently established intermediate care and reablement services, including residential units funded and operated jointly with NHS partners; short-term extra care housing provision; and domiciliary reablement services. The latter services had involved reorganising social services departments' in-house services to provide short-term interventions, free of charge, to improve older people's mobility, independence and confidence, with longer-term domiciliary support commissioned from independent providers.

One site had restructured its in-house home care service to provide short-term rehabilitation-oriented interventions for *all* new service users. Following referral, the team, which included an occupational therapist, identified a user's desired change outcomes; the older person received support for up to six weeks; and progress towards desired outcomes was reviewed at weekly meetings. Front-line staff were encouraged to provide feedback on the appropriateness of the care plan and also have some autonomy over how they delivered care on a daily basis.

Another site had developed outcomes-based contract specifications for a new range of preventive services. These included assessment and rehabilitation services in residential and extra care housing settings; and a multidisciplinary community reablement team working in older people's homes to promote independence, focusing on goals that were important to the individual, for up to eight weeks (although this could be extended if necessary to achieve individual goals). The service was free of charge; staff considered that charges deterred take-up and were inappropriate for a service that encouraged users to do things for themselves.

Commissioning for maintenance outcomes – independent providers

Three study sites had changed their contracts with independent home care providers to facilitate outcomes-focused services. These changes involved a delicate balance between:

- flexibility to respond to users
- predictability in workloads, expenditure (by purchasers and service users) and income (for providers)
- audit and payment arrangements that were not unduly onerous and expensive.

In one rural site, each home care provider now worked in a specific geographical 'zone'. Although this reduced the choice of provider for service users, there were distinct gains for staff recruitment and retention and in continuity of relationships with users. Because a given level of work could be guaranteed for each provider, invoicing was done on a four-week standing order-style arrangement, based on the estimated annual workload and adjusted periodically to account for the actual time spent. This gave providers flexibility to deal with unexpected situations without having first to contact care managers.

Another rural locality was also piloting a 'zoned' approach. Providers were to work in the areas where they currently had greatest presence; each will have a block contract with social services to provide a core level of home care services in that zone. Care managers were to specify in care plans the tasks users required help with and the probable number of hours of help required (this also provided the basis for the client's financial assessment). Providers would notify social services each week of the actual hours they delivered against what was ordered. Users would not be billed for any extra help they received unless it became regular, in which case it could trigger a reassessment and a new order for the home care provider.

This arrangement is expected to create some 'down time', when provider staff have spare hours. Social workers will be asked to identify in advance older people who would benefit from practical help (for example, with housework or going out) and down time will be used for this; again, users will not pay for this extra help. Providers expect this will enable them to employ staff on a shift basis; to guarantee a minimum amount of work each week; and to arrange staff training (including training on outcomes) during any 'down time'.

Contributors to the Better Commissioning LIN suggested three models of outcome-based commissioning:

Three models of outcome-based commissioning

Following assessment of eligibility and identification of desired outcomes:

- Care managers allocate blocks of hours to providers for a group of service users; providers have autonomy to allocate these to individual users depending on their circumstances and priorities.
- Care managers specify the number of hours normally to be received by each service user, but providers have flexibility to move hours between people according to need.
- Care managers allocate a specified number of hours to each service user who has freedom to use these in whatever way s/he wishes.

We could find only one example (from the Better Commissioning LIN) of an outcomes-based approach to commissioning home care services that had been evaluated.

Outcome-based home care commissioning: evaluation of pilot project

In this pilot project, care managers agreed outcomes and an appropriate budget for each home care service user and let the provider negotiate the details with the user, with sufficient autonomy to respond flexibly to needs and preferences. The care plan and assessment summary set out the outcomes that the provider was expected to achieve. The service user plan set out the activities to be carried out to achieve these outcomes and the estimated number of hours required. Seventy service users were included in the pilot: 19 per cent received maintenance-based outcomes services and 81 per cent received change outcomes services. Local evaluation of the pilot found higher levels of user satisfaction than in a recent national user experience survey and increased job satisfaction was reported by front-line home care staff. Only eight per cent of care packages exceeded the original budget. A number of learning points were identified, including:

- providers need an appropriate infrastructure to be able to construct, cost and adapt service user plans as necessary
- care managers must be confident that providers can match activities to outcomes and will monitor users regularly. Good communication between providers and care managers was essential
- revisions to paperwork and financial processes were needed to improve communication and reduce paperwork
- new contracts should include performance management frameworks defining the council's and provider's respective responsibilities for monitoring; frameworks should incorporate key performance indicators.

Case study sites involved in outcomes-based commissioning of independent home care services agreed they involve transferring power and responsibility from commissioners to providers and users. This required significant levels of trust between purchasers and providers; open communication channels; and appropriate administrative and financial management systems.

Although these new approaches to commissioning could result in less choice of provider for service users, members of the User Advisory Group did not consider this a problem. They were concerned at the transfer of home care services from in-house to independent agencies as they felt that this gave them less control over the quality, reliability and costs of services. The costs of home care services were also perceived to be a barrier for some older people. Moreover, if home care services were to be provided by independent agencies, Advisory Group members did not want the responsibility of choosing an agency themselves; indeed, they considered choice to be meaningless without access to information and support.

One case study site had experience of commissioning low-level preventive services from local voluntary groups. In this locality, Age Concern was contracted to organise a volunteer shopping and home de-livery service. Age Concern had enhanced its basic service by producing lists of local shops that will deliver and by offering advice on internet shopping. In another part of the locality, Age Concern provided a short-term volunteer service to fill gaps in statutory services for older people at risk of hospital admission (for example, help with laundry and shopping or looking after pets).

2.3.3 Outcomes-focused services

2.3.3.1 Intermediate care and 'reablement' services

Early discussions in several case study sites led the research team to focus on intermediate care and reablement services, as staff thought these showed greatest progress in outcomes-focused approaches. These services have a very clear focus on change outcomes.

Typically, reablement services aim to promote independence by iden-tifying and working towards outcomes that were important to each individual. Domiciliary reablement services were thought to give added encouragement to a holistic approach. For example, initial referrals iden-tified goals that users wished to achieve and these are refined during an initial assessment visit from the team's occupational therapist. Goals might relate to personal care, daily living activities such as shopping or leisure interests – 'We try to tailor things very much to what the client says'. Subsequently a detailed picture of the user and her/his desired out-comes was compiled; this was shared with rehabilitation assistants who visited regularly. In one site, users could request visits at times to fit their daily routines (the service could be offered seven days a week between 7am and 10pm). Visits were arranged a week in advance and a timetable sent to users every Friday so they know who to expect and when.

Outcomes could include, for example, going shopping or attending art classes. Helping to restore confidence in whatever areas of life are important to users was central. In one area, progress was measured using the Canadian Occupational Performance Measure that is both person-centred and outcomes-focused. It asks about a user's lifestyle and what is important to them; identifies the top five things they want to do; asks how satisfied users are currently with their ability to do these things; and then asks again after a period of intervention. Smiley faces can be used for people with cognitive impairments and interpreters for people who do not speak English.

2.3.3.2 Day care

One locality was reviewing its output-based contracts for voluntary sector day care services, to see if new incentives to focus on user outcomes could be introduced. In another day centre for older people with mental health problems, a six-week assessment period allowed staff to identify users' individual interests; each user was then assigned a key worker who shared their interests, so the focus on outcomes was as natural as possible. However, no examples were found of day services that addressed outcomes that could be met other than by attendance at a day centre.

2.3.3.3 Residential and nursing home care

A Quality Development Scheme (QDS) had been developed by one locality for its 40 nursing and residential homes, to encourage standards above the CSCI minimum. Homes receiving the QDS Award received an additional payment for each local authority-funded resident and a marketing advantage as they were clearly flagged up on the local authority's website. In addition, residential care staff could attend outcomes training run by social services, although staffing constraints restricted take-up.

2.3.4 Monitoring and evaluation

The most frequent and systematic monitoring of user outcomes appeared to occur in relation to the change outcomes that were the focus of intermediate care and reablement services. For example, clinical outcome tools were often used; weekly reviews and six-weekly reviews of users were routinely conducted; and questionnaires obtained feedback from users at the end of their first week in a rehabilitation unit and again on discharge.

In contrast, little evidence was found of routine monitoring of maintenance and prevention outcomes among long-term users of home care services. One authority was considering how to include user outcomes in its new arrangements for monitoring home care providers, but had not yet done so. In another case study site that had a long-standing commitment to outcomes-focused assessment and care management, information from outcomes-focused assessment documents was not available electronically and could therefore not be aggregated and used as part of the monitoring and contracting arrangements with independent providers. Managers here noted that as outcomes were not a national priority or performance target, organisational resources to develop appropriate computer information systems were a low priority. However, in another authority centralised contracting for independent home care services enabled the feedback from annual reviews of service users to be incorporated into strategic planning.

In relation to monitoring outcomes in residential homes, managers identified multiple opportunities to obtain feedback from users:

Monitoring and evaluation in residential care settings

- Feedback from residents' monthly meetings
- Quality Circles of resident, relative and staff representatives that met monthly to discuss performance and areas for improvement
- Routine questionnaires, for example about meals, privacy
- Annual surveys of residents, relatives, staff and GPs
- Suggestion boxes
- Managers being easily accessible to residents
- Feedback from routine audits (for example, kitchens, accidents)
- Information from performance indicators

2.3.5 Impact of outcomes-focused services: the experiences of service users

This section reports the views of older service users who took part in interviews and focus groups in the case study sites.

2.3.5.1 Change outcomes

These were particularly evident in intermediate care and reablement services. Many users reported changes in their morale and outlook on life as well as their physical functioning, thus supporting staff claims to take a holistic approach.

> Miss B had a fall and broke her hip. On leaving hospital her mobility was greatly reduced, partly because she lacked confidence to walk outside in case she fell again. She was therefore unable to do her shopping and maintain her social life. After referral to intermediate care, she received physiotherapy, equipment and support from a rehabilitation assistant to regain her confidence. 'I wouldn't be where I am now – mobile and with confidence – without it'.
>
> One older person celebrated a small milestone in her rehabilitation – being able to clean the toilet independently: 'I really enjoyed that!'
>
> Mr F spent several weeks in a rehabilitation unit after a hospital stay. He said that staff in the unit had a very personal approach and understood what was important to him. 'One of my aims was to walk the dog, so they allowed him to come and see me – it was very helpful.... It made all the difference in the world.... I have a good quality of life and I know I can get better still.... You need to look forward – they kept stressing that – and I'm the living proof!'

Staff working in reablement services pointed out that, as older people regain their abilities and confidence in relation to self-care and household activities, desired outcomes change rapidly – goals that originally seemed unattainable soon become realistic. Regular reassessment was therefore important. They also pointed out that even where significant change outcomes had been achieved, these were not always maintained when older people moved to longer-term home care services: 'It gets so far then it's out of our hands and we can't follow it through'.

2.3.5.2 Maintenance outcomes

It was harder to find examples of maintenance outcomes. Some managers acknowledged this lack of evidence reflected services commissioned from independent home care agencies that prioritised physical maintenance rather than broader quality of life outcomes. Interviews with older people confirmed that some outcomes that were important to them, such as going out, participating in social activities and help with housework, were not being addressed by home care services.

However, older people did give examples of day and residential care services that met desired maintenance outcomes:

Mrs R used to be very active in her local community. After a hospital stay she received home care but, as she felt isolated and bored, she started attending a day centre. One of her desired outcomes was to keep socially involved; she enjoyed the range of day centre activities and appreciated the time staff spent finding out about her interests in theatre and music so they could match activities to these.

In one combined residential and day care facility for Asian elders, users acknowledged the importance of the social participation in maintaining morale: 'I think it's great ... you can sit down and have a chat and a giggle – it's a change.' 'I didn't want to come here at first but I'm glad I did now – it gives you something to look forward to.' 'It's lonely in the flat ... you get company here.'

Day centre users in another site appreciated the variety of activities available – 'There's something for everyone'. They could influence the activities provided and confirmed senior managers' claims of an open culture – what one user described as a 'No secrets policy'.

Care home residents appreciated the choice and control they could exercise: 'There's a elderly lady in here that said [about another home] once you come out of your room you've got to stay in the lounge, whereas here I go to [friend]'s room, I go and sit and have a yarn with her'.

2.3.5.3 Process outcomes

These were more often noted by users of intermediate care and reablement services, day care and residential care than by users of long-term home care services. In one locality with a high proportion of minority ethnic elders, Asian older people attending day centres valued having staff who spoke their languages: 'They make you feel good ... you're well looked after'. 'They make you feel like one of the family, not a senior citizen.' An older person attending another day centre praised the 'team spirit' among staff, which extended to the bus driver who took her into her living room and drew the curtains for her when he took her home on dark evenings.

Care home residents reflected on their experience of process outcomes:

'The senior carers are good, they listen, which means a lot. They are caring and they understand.'

'[The manager is] very warm, very considerate ... involved every day in every way.'

A care home resident didn't sleep well. When she was awake during the night, staff looked in on her and brought a cup of tea.

The next morning she was able to lie in and staff brought her breakfast to her room on a tray.

Users of intermediate care services recognised the importance of process outcomes, both for the acceptability of the service and in underpinning change outcomes.

One resident described her therapy timetable as 'fluid' and 'flexible.... You can do what you prefer. You have control, you're not regimented and that all helps to regain your independence'.

Mrs S was discharged from hospital after a hip fracture. She was reluctant to accept intermediate care because she 'didn't want to be taken over by strangers coming into the house'. However, once back home, a rehabilitation assistant worked with her to devise safe ways to do domestic tasks. Running her home was very important to Mrs S and the intermediate care team understood this: 'Some people say "We want you to do this or that", but they weren't like that.... They didn't intrude on your life like some do-gooders do'.

Mrs H spent four weeks in residential intermediate care following discharge from hospital. She reflected 'They [staff] taught me to stand on my own two feet – I knew that was their aim. It wasn't just physical, it was emotional. They were really wonderful, they really listened, everything I mentioned they discussed. They got to know me and to understand what my aims were. The staff were never abrupt, you never felt I was in the way. I gradually started to feel better ... I started doing things for myself.'

Members of the User Advisory Group endorsed the importance for process outcomes of individualised, personalised approaches, underpinned by good staff training.

2.3.5.4 Service-level outcomes

As in the postal survey, some managers and practitioners also referred to outcomes for services, not just for users. A significant driver behind the development of outcomes-focused intermediate care and reablement services was to reduce hospital and residential care admissions; staff therefore reported major gains in enabling older people to live independently. These sometimes also included a significant decrease in residential care admissions that generated additional resources for community services. A further impact reported by several sites was increased staff satisfaction and, consequently, improved recruitment and retention, particularly in relation to rehabilitation assistant posts that were more rewarding (both psychologically and financially) than care assistant posts. However, this had implications for the staffing of long-term home care services.

2.3.5.5 Constraints on the impact of outcomes-focused approaches

Staff and users both identified constraints on the impact of outcomes-focused initiatives. Mostly these related to the quality and range of home care services, which could limit or even reverse change outcomes resulting from a period of intensive reablement. Intermediate care staff in one area tried to plan for change outcomes to be maintained when older people returned home, but found long-term services could not sustain the same personalised, enabling approach. Older people confirmed that some desired outcomes, such as resuming social activities, were not being met. Day centre users in another site reported restrictions in maintaining valued social activities outside the day centre as they could not get out without help.

2.3.6 Factors facilitating outcomes approaches

2.3.6.1 National policies

Case study interviewees confirmed the findings of the postal survey, that outcomes approaches were increasingly compatible with the national policy environment. Relevant policies included:

- the NSF for older people
- policy pressures and dedicated resources to reduce hospital and residential care admissions; sometimes adverse CSCI inspections of a local authority's role in relation to delayed hospital discharges had prompted the development of new, in-house reablement services
- the promotion of greater user choice and control through direct payments
- the Green Paper on adult social care
- some interviewees also thought that CSCI inspections of residential and home care services had become less paper-driven and more compatible with outcomes approaches.

The development of intermediate care services, both in partnership with NHS colleagues and in-house, were particularly significant factors, as they involved dedicated funding and the creation of new teams with a strong focus on change outcomes, underpinned by a person-centred culture. The importance of compatible performance indicators – inevitably 'a big part of a manager's working life' – in promoting outcomes approaches was emphasised several times.

Several sites had been involved in SPRU's Outcomes Network and this had provided important opportunities to share ideas with others. Other national networks that had helped included the Modernisation Agency's Accelerated Development Programme and the Innovations Forum.

2.3.6.2 Local vision, leadership and investment in change management

Leadership was essential. This needed to come from senior managers who wanted, were in a position to and had time to devote to managing change: 'You can't do it as part of your day job – you need thinking time'. Sometimes senior managers were new appointees who brought a new vision of person-centred services; sometimes they were long-standing members of staff who identified new opportunities to introduce change. In one or two instances political leadership was also noted as a significant enabling factor.

A 'whole systems' approach to managing change was important, as were clear communication channels to 'take the staff with you' so that 'we're all swimming the same way'. Examples included:

- regular meetings between commissioning and care management teams and between all assessment and care management staff to keep them involved in change processes
- regular workshops for residential home staff to reinforce cultural change
- formal staff training in using outcomes-focused documents
- induction, training and on-going supervision for day centre staff
- 'back to the floor' sessions by senior managers who carried out home visits with staff
- having care plans 'signed off' by senior and principal care managers who could spot and talk through any 'mistakes'. Sometimes a new care manager had a senior colleague working alongside to help embed an outcomes approach when drawing up care plans.

2.3.6.3 Partnerships and whole systems working

Close relationships with external partners were essential to implementing outcomes approaches. Outcomes-focused intermediate care and reablement services required close collaboration with NHS partners. Other partners included voluntary organisations, particularly in providing day care and low-level preventive services; and independent home care providers, for successful outcomes-focused approaches to contracting for domiciliary care.

At operational levels, integrated services improved access to a wider range of skills and resources to meet users' outcomes. The success of this multidisciplinary approach was particularly apparent in intermediate and day care services. Activities to promote interdisciplinary working included joint training, regular meetings, shared accommodation and staff secondments. However, 'outcomes' could have different meanings for medical and social care professionals and debates about 'medical' versus 'social' models had impeded the development of integrated, outcomes-focused day services in one site. A 'whole systems' approach also required appropriate administrative and computerised information systems. Training in outcomes-focused approaches was often linked to the introduction of new (electronic or hard copy) documentation.

Members of the User Advisory Group also pointed to the support that other professionals and services could provide, including specialist NHS units for older people with mental health problems and community nursing staff. For housebound older people, regular visits from community nurses could be as important for their social as their clinical functions, as they addressed maintenance outcomes relating to social contact.

Although some localities reported extensive multi-agency working, it was not clear how this contributed specifically to delivering outcomes-focused services. However, as noted above, partnerships with voluntary organisations such as Age Concern to provide a range of low-level services aimed at maintenance and prevention outcomes were common.

2.3.7 What hinders outcomes approaches?

2.3.7.1 National policies and performance indicators

Although some localities had adapted care planning and review documents to overcome the needs focus of SAP, this was not entirely successful. Keeping SAP focused on outcomes was described as a 'constant battle': home care service managers thought it focused too much on medical conditions; day centre staff described it as 'something to be endured' rather than a process that enhanced an outcomes approach.

Other policies also impeded outcomes-focused services:

- CSCI inspection regimes were thought still to be too paper based, as were registration requirements that did not value staff experience sufficiently
- pressures to reduce delayed hospital discharges had reduced opportunities to identify and achieve desired discharge outcomes for some patients
- in poorly performing authorities, a preoccupation with improving performance indicators detracted from developing outcomes approaches.

2.3.7.2 Resource constraints

These had a number of impacts:

- resources were not available for voluntary organisations to provide low-level preventive services to address maintenance outcomes

- constraints on NHS budgets threatened access to services like chiropody and physiotherapy that were vital in helping older people achieve desired change and maintenance outcomes
- resource panels that approved care managers' recommendations could prevent outcomes-focused care plans from being fully implemented
- workload pressures reduced care managers' capacity to adopt a holistic and individualised approach
- resource constraints could restrict outcomes-focused contracts with independent home care providers, especially where these needed to be flexible and open-ended. These constraints could be exacerbated by poor relationships with home care providers
- resource constraints restricted home care providers in recruiting, training and retaining good quality staff.

2.3.7.3 Staff culture and attitudes

- Previous resource constraints could leave a legacy on staff culture and attitudes so that earlier, less flexible care planning practices were hard to change
- Social services commissioners reported some home care staff found it difficult to keep up with rapid service modernisation and move from doing everything for an older person to letting them decide on their priorities and working with them to achieve these
- Problems with the attitudes and practices of other professional groups could impede outcomes approaches, again highlighting the importance of 'whole systems' approaches. For example, some GPs were reported still to advise older people that residential care was the 'only option', although allocating social services staff to GP practices could help change this practice. Some sheltered housing wardens also continued to assume that residential care was a preferred outcome. Hospital staff involved in discharge planning also had difficulty understanding concepts of outcomes and prevention.

2.3.7.4 Users' and carers' attitudes

Users and carers were sometimes resistant to outcomes-focused approaches. Problems included deference and a reluctance to articulate desired outcomes for fear of appearing unrealistic. Managers explained this as a legacy of previous experiences of services: 'Users find it hard to understand choice – they were so used to having services shoved on them'. Some older people were resistant to a reablement approach as they were said to be used to people 'coming and doing things'. Other users resisted the withdrawal of time-limited home reablement services, even if desired change outcomes had been achieved.

Users' desired outcomes could conflict with those of carers, especially when the latter placed more emphasis on safety while the older person was prepared to accept a greater level of risk in order to maintain independence. Differences in attitudes to risk had to be tackled through 'good social work', to reinforce the older person's preferences while helping the family to distinguish between unconventional and dangerous behaviours.

2.3.8 Plans for (further) outcomes-focused service developments

All the case study sites had plans to build on or extend outcomes approaches to other services, activities or localities. These plans reflected local priorities and circumstances and included the following activities.

2.3.8.1 Consolidating previous outcomes work

One county authority aimed to achieve a consistent outcomes focus across all its services by revising its commissioning strategy to include closer links with local older people's organisations; promoting take-up of direct payments; and continuing to develop as many joint services as possible with NHS partners. These objectives were acknowledged to be challenging in the context of high workloads and staff shortages.

A priority for localities with high staff turnover was to 'relaunch' outcomes with a new series of training sessions. In other localities, priorities included increasing the volume of short-term reablement services, and working with partner organisations (including hospital consultants, independent providers and carers) to extend understanding of outcomes.

2.3.8.2 Extending outcomes approaches into new services

Some localities planned to extend their outcomes approaches by developing new specifications and contracts for services such as extra care housing, day care, residential care and dementia care that had hitherto not had an outcomes focus. One locality planned to build on its relatively stable workforce and comparatively long tradition of outcomes-focused approaches by incorporating outcomes into the SAP; and by reviewing its contracting and service standards processes to ensure they did not impede outcomes approaches.

New contracts with independent home care providers were a priority for some sites. Proposed changes included retendering for larger, locality-based block contracts with a smaller number of providers; and ensuring that all new contracts had flexible, outcomes-focused specifications.

2.3.8.3 Developing preventive services

Some localities had identified a major gap in low-level services that could address the prevention and maintenance outcomes valued by older people. Filling this gap was challenging and involved identifying new sources of funding and labour. Two localities had successfully bid for POPPs. One of these localities intended to promote community development approaches to strengthen the role of local neighbourhoods and community organisations in supporting older people; older people themselves were expected to play a key role in identifying, articulating and addressing local needs and concerns. Linked to this ambition were plans to seek EU funding to employ older people themselves as care staff to provide low-level support. Developing local networks of older people was also intended to enable older people's perspectives on local needs to inform service commissioners; indeed, it was planned that the latter would be accountable to the locality-wide POPP.

Another locality planned to enable care managers to access local sources of help and support:

Bridging the gap between care managers and local services

One locality was relocating all its care managers from a central office to ward level; each would be given a laptop computer and mobile phone. Locally based care managers were expected to be able to make better links with local communities and with the informal, neighbourhood and voluntary resources in them; this would in turn provide access to a wider range of support options – for example, providing a taxi to a local community event rather than having to be transported to a distant day centre simply because care managers did not know what else was available. It was also hoped that the new local base would encourage care managers to proactively 'case find' older people who might benefit from low-level preventive work.

Conclusions

During the past decade, discussion of outcomes has become common, as part of a wider service modernisation discourse.

As well as the SPRU Outcomes Programme, other policy initiatives have promoted outcomes-focused services. First, this practice survey shows that targeted funding and performance indicators related to hospital discharge and intermediate care have produced significant developments in services focused on change outcomes. Moreover, these are not restricted to NHS and social services intermediate care, rapid response and 'step-down' services; but are also increasingly reflected in social services' in-house home care services that provide short-term reablement-oriented interventions.

Second, the policy emphasis on prevention means that in some areas efforts are being made to develop low-level services, often through partnerships with voluntary and community organisations. These may contribute to meeting valued maintenance outcomes such as domestic help and social participation. These initiatives are likely to develop further as POPPs pilots get under way. Third, inspection and quality indicators for residential and day care services appear to have had an impact on process outcomes, at least according to the service users interviewed in this survey. Many of these process outcomes also feature strongly in older people's experiences of rehabilitation and reablement services.

Overall, it is increasingly difficult to identify a distinctive social care 'outcomes' focus. Many of the outcomes desired by older people are likely to be addressed as the result of other policies and service developments. Thus in the case study interviews, managers and front-line practitioners did not always use the language of outcomes but referred as well to goals, independence, prevention or person-centred services. Members of the User Advisory Group also noted the contributions of other organisations and services, particularly NHS staff and voluntary sector organisations, to desired outcomes.

However, there remain some significant gaps. The overall impression, even from case study sites chosen for their outcome-related approaches, is one of fragmentation. The outcomes valued by older people were most likely to be achieved in services with strong interprofessional teams and devolved resources over which they had control. For example, in multidisciplinary reablement services, day centres and residential care homes, staff had access to a range of skills and resources that they could draw on flexibly in response to users' priorities and to changes in these. However, there appeared to be significant disjunctions between these examples of good practice and service users' wider lives. For example, day centres could provide excellent quality services, with a high emphasis on process outcomes, for those who attended. However, support for users to maintain their own social networks outside the day centre was non-existent.

The most striking disjunction, acknowledged by many managers and practitioners, was between short-term reablement services and longer-term home care services. Here resource constraints and poor relationships with independent providers meant that home care services were often inflexible, of poor quality and insufficiently responsive to the outcomes desired by older users. The new contracting arrangements described in this knowledge review are in their very early stages and need careful monitoring and evaluation to ensure they deliver home care services that address maintenance and process outcomes.

As with any major organisational change, introducing an outcomes focus into social care requires leadership and vision; the means to communicate effectively to all staff; and the capacity to underpin cultural change with appropriate procedural and information management arrangements. For all the case study sites in this practice survey, the SAP constituted a barrier rather than an enabling factor and managers had struggled to make it compatible with outcomes-focused approaches.

The outcomes desired by older people extend beyond the support currently provided by social services departments. Partnerships – with health, other local authority services such as transport, and particularly with voluntary sector organisations that appear increasingly to be providing low-level preventive services – are therefore key to outcomes-focused approaches. Members of the User Advisory Group also emphasised that many of the wider, life-enhancing outcomes valued by older people extend beyond the scope of social services. Close relationships with voluntary organisations were considered to be key to filling some of these gaps. However, members stressed that voluntary organisations must have adequate funding and flexibility to play this role, rather than be constrained by rigid contracts with their local authorities. Securely funded advocacy schemes were also considered essential in supporting older people to identify desired outcomes and to access the services needed to fulfil these outcomes.

It is therefore important that the policy priority and resources allocated to intermediate care services that promote change and process outcomes do not eclipse the continuing need for low-level services that promote preventive and maintenance outcomes. It is significant that managers and users interviewed in the practice survey made very little mention of alternative forms of delivering support such as direct payments or individual budgets. It is therefore likely that, for older people at least, a significant challenge remains for social services departments to develop and sustain their different relationships with those voluntary and independent providers who can supply the outcomes-related support that older people need.

References

[1] Leadbeater, C. (2004) *Personalisation through participation: A new script for public services*, London: Demos.

[2] Department of Health (2005) *Independence, well-being and choice: Our vision for the future of social care in England*, Cm 6499, London: DH.

[3] Department for Work and Pensions (2005) *Opportunity age*, London: DWP.

[4] Walker, A. and Hennessy, C. (2004) *Growing older: Quality of life in old age*, Maidenhead: Open University Press.

[5] Parry, J., Vegeris, S., Hudson, M., Barnes, H. and Taylor, R. (2004) *Independent living in later life*, Research Report 216, London: DWP.

[6] Audit Commission (2004) *Older people – Independence and well-being. The challenge for public services*, London: Audit Commission.

[7] Baldock, J.C. and Hadlow, J. (2001) *How older people sustain their identities and preferences in the face of a limited physical condition and the need to accept health and care services*, Growing Older Programme, Swindon: ESRC.

[8] Bajekal, M., Blane, D., Grewal, I., Karlsen, S. and Nazroo, J. (2004) 'Ethnic differences in influences on quality of life at older ages: a quantitative analysis', *Ageing and Society*, no 24, pp 709–728.

[9] Ware, T., Matosevic, T., Hardy, B., Knapp, M., Kendall, J. and Forder, J. (2003) 'Commissioning care services for older people in England: the view from care managers, users and carers', *Ageing and Society*, no 23, pp 411–428.

[10] Parry-Jones, B. and Soulsby, J. (2001) 'Needs-led assessment: the challenges and the reality', *Health and Social Care in the Community*, no 9, pp 414–428.

[11] Qureshi, H., Patmore, C., Nicholas, E. and Bamford, C. (1998) *Outcomes in community care practice. Overview: Outcomes of social care for older people and carers*, Report No 5, York: Social Policy Research Unit, University of York.

[12] Qureshi, H. and Henwood, M. (2000) *Older people's definitions of quality services*, York: Joseph Rowntree Foundation.

[13] Raynes, N. (1998) 'Involving residents in quality specification', *Ageing and Society*, no 18, pp 65–78.

[14] Gwyther, L. (1997) 'The perspective of the person with Alzheimer disease: which outcomes matter in early to middle stage of dementia?', *Alzheimer Disease and Related Disorders*, no 11, pp 18–24.

[15] Clark, H., Dyer, S. and Horwood, J. (1998) *'That bit of help': The high value of low level preventative services for older people*, Bristol: The Policy Press.

[16] Joseph Rowntree Foundation (2003) 'Social service users' own definitions of quality outcomes', Report on Shaping Our Lives Project, Ref 673 (available at www.jrf.org.uk, June).

[17] Gabriel, Z. and Bowling, A. (2004) 'Quality of life from the perspectives of older people', *Ageing and Society*, no 24, pp 675–692.

[18] Clark, H., Gough, H. and Macfarlane, A. (2004) *'It pays dividends': Direct payments and older people*, Bristol/York: The Policy Press/Joseph Rowntree Foundation.

[19] Godfrey, M. and Callaghan, G. (2000) *Exploring unmet need: The challenge of a user-centred response*, York: Joseph Rowntree Foundation.

[20] Wenger, C. (1992) *Help in old age: Facing up to change*, Liverpool: Liverpool University Press.

[21] Coleman, P.G., Ivani-Chalian, C. and Robinson, M. (1998) 'The story continues: persistence of life themes in old age', *Ageing and Society*, no 18, pp 398–419.

[22] Henwood, M., Lewis, H. and Waddington, E. (1998) *Listening to users of domiciliary care services*, Leeds: Community Care Division, Nuffield Institute for Health, University of Leeds.

[23] Bamford, C. and Bruce, E. (2000) 'Defining the outcomes of community care: the perspectives of older people with dementia', *Ageing and Society*, no 20, pp 543–570.

[24] Godlove Mozley, C., Sutcliffe, C., Bagley, H., Cordingley, L., Huxley, P., Challis, D. and Burns, A. (2000) 'The quality of life study: outcomes for older people in nursing and residential homes', Unpublished report presented to the NHS Executive, London: DH.

[25] Cordingley, L., Hughes, J. and Challis, D. (2001) *Unmet need and older people: Towards a synthesis of user and provider views*, York: Joseph Rowntree Foundation.

[26] Patmore, C. (2003) *Understanding home care providers: Live issues about management, quality and relationships with social services purchasers*, Working Paper No DH 1963, York: Social Policy Research Unit, University of York.

[27] Beaumont, G. and Kenealy, P. (2004) 'Quality of life perceptions and social comparisons in healthy old age', *Ageing and Society*, no 24, pp 755–770.

[28] Audit Commission (1997) *The coming of age: Improving care services for older people*, London: Audit Commission.

[29] Joseph Rowntree Foundation (2004) 'Older people shaping policy and practice', Summary of 18 research projects, Ref 044 (available at www.jrf.org.uk/knowledge/findings/foundations/044.asp, October).

[30] Cordingley, L. (1999) 'Relationships between health, social support and independence in older people: a study using the SF-36 and Q methodology', Unpublished PhD thesis, University of Manchester.

[31] Tester, S., Hubbard, G., Downs, M., MacDonald, C. and Murphy, J. (2003) *Exploring perceptions of quality of life of frail older people during and after their transition to institutional care*, Research Findings 24, Growing Older Programme, Swindon: ESRC.

[32] Hayden, C., Boaz, A. and Taylor, F. (1999) *Attitudes and aspirations of older people: A qualitative study*, Research Report 102, London: DWP.

[33] Shaping Our Lives Project (2003) *Shaping Our Lives: From outset to outcome: What people think of the social care services they use*, York: Joseph Rowntree Foundation and the DH.

[34] Francis, J. and Netten, A. (2004) 'Raising the quality of home care: a study of service users' views', *Social Policy and Administration*, no 38, pp 290–305.

[35] Qureshi, H. (1999) 'Outcomes of social care for adults: attitudes towards collecting outcome information in practice', *Health and Social Care in the Community*, no 7, pp 257–265.

[36] Francis, J. and Netten, A. (2002) *Homecare services in one local authority: Client and provider views*, Rep 1795/3, London: Personal Social Services Research Unit.

[37] Boaz, A., Hayden, C. and Bernard, M. (1999) *Attitudes and aspirations of older people: A review of the literature*, Research Report 101, London: DWP.

38 Netten, A., Ryan, M., Smith, P., Skatun, D., Healey, A., Knapp, M. and Wykes, T. (2002) *The development of a measure of social care outcome for older people*, Rep PSSRU Discussion Paper 1690/2, University of Kent: Personal Social Services Research Unit.

39 Willis, M., Douglas, G. and Pavey, S. (2005) 'Defining vision', *Community Care*, 7–13 July, pp 32–33.

40 Askham, J., Henshaw, L. and Tarpey, M. (1995) *Social and health authority services for elderly people from black and minority ethnic communities*, London: HMSO.

41 Mold, F., Fitzpatrick, J.M. and Roberts, J.D. (2005) 'Minority ethnic elders in care homes: a review of the literature', *Age and Ageing*, vol 34, no 2, pp 107–113.

42 Butt, J. and Mirza, K. (1996) *Social care and black communities*, London: The Stationery Office.

43 Allan, K. (2001) *Communication and consultation: Exploring ways for staff to involve people with dementia in developing services*, Bristol: The Policy Press.

44 Patel, N., Mirza, N., Linbland, P., Amstrup, K. and Samaoh, O. (1998) *Dementia and minority ethnic older people. Managing care in the UK, Denmark and France*, Lyme Regis: Russell House Publishing.

45 Ramcharan, P., Grant, G., Parry-Jones, B. and Robinson, C. (1999) 'The roles and tasks of care management practitioners in Wales revisited', *Managing Community Care*, no 7, pp 29–36.

46 Challis, D., Weiner, K., Darton, R., Hughes, J. and Stewart, K. (2001) 'Emerging patterns of care management: arrangements for older people in England', *Social Policy and Administration*, no 35, pp 672–687.

47 Quinn, A., Snowling, A. and Denicolo, P. (2003) *Older people's perspectives: Devising information, advice and advocacy services*, York: Joseph Rowntree Foundation.

48 Baldock, J.C. and Hadlow, J. (2002) 'Self-talk versus needs-talk: an exploration of the priorities of housebound older people', *Quality in Ageing: Policy, Practice and Research*, no 3, pp 42–49.

49 Godfrey, M. and Moore, J. (1996) *Hospital discharge: User, carer and professional perspectives*, Leeds: Nuffield Institute for Health, University of Leeds.

50 Clark, H., Dyer, S. and Hartman, L. (1996) *Going home: Older people leaving hospital*, Bristol: The Policy Press.

51 Age Concern (2006) *The Age Agenda 2006: Public policy and older people*, London: Age Concern.

52 Hardy, B., Young, R. and Wistow, G. (1999) 'Dimensions of choice in the assessment and care management process: the views of older people, carers and care managers', *Health and Social Care in the Community*, no 7, pp 483–491.

53 Boneham, M.A., Williams, K.E. and Copeland, J.R.M. (1997) 'Elderly people from ethnic minorities in Liverpool: mental illness, unmet need and barriers to service use', *Health and Social Care in the Community*, vol 5, no 3, pp 173–180.

54 Nocon, A. and Qureshi, H. (1996) *Outcomes of community care for service users and carers: A social services perspective*, Report No 2, York: Social Policy Research Unit, University of York.

55 Department of Health (2001) *Social services performance assessment framework indicators 2000–2001*, London: DH.

56 Sinclair, I., Gibbs, I. and Hicks, L. (2000) *The management and effectiveness of the home care service*, York: Social Work Research and Development Unit, University of York.

57 Patmore, C. and McNulty, A. (2005) *Making home care for older people more flexible and person-centred: Factors which promote this*, Working Paper No DH 2069, York: Social Policy Research Unit, University of York.

58 Forder, J., Knapp, M., Hardy, B., Kendall, J., Matosevic, T. and Ware, P. (2004) 'Prices, contracts and motivations: institutional arrangements in domiciliary care', *Policy & Politics*, no 32, pp 207–222.

59 Knapp, M., Hardy, B. and Forder, J. (2001) 'Commissioning for quality: ten years of social care markets', *Journal of Social Policy*, no 30, pp 283–306.

60 Matosevic, T., Ware, P., Forder, J., Hardy, B., Kendall, J., Knapp, M. and Wistow, G. (2000) *Independent sector domiciliary sector providers in 1999*, London: Personal Social Services Research Unit, London School of Economics and Political Science.

61 Kendall, J., Matosevic, T., Forder, J., Knapp, M., Hardy, B. and Ware, P. (2003) 'The motivations of domiciliary care providers in England: new concepts, new findings', *Journal of Social Policy*, vol 32, no 4, pp 489–511.

62 Social Services Inspectorate (1999) *Of primary importance: Inspection of social services departments' links with primary health services*, London: DH.

63 Health Advisory Service (1997) *Services for people who are elderly: Addressing the balance*, London: The Stationery Office.

64 Banerjee, S. and Macdonald, A. (1996) 'Mental disorder in an elderly home care population: associations with health and social services use', *British Journal of Psychiatry*, vol 168, pp 760–766.

65 Schneider, J. (1997) *Quality of care: Testing some measures in homes for elderly people*, Discussion Paper 1245, Canterbury: Personal Social Services Research Unit, University of Kent.

66 Alexopoulos, G. (1996) 'Editorial: geriatric depression in primary care', *International Journal of Geriatric Psychiatry*, no 11, pp 397–400.

67 Patel, N. (1998) 'Black and minority ethnic elderly: perspectives on long-term care', in *With respect to old age; Research volume 1, Royal Commission on Long-term Care*, London: The Stationery Office.

68 Qureshi, H. (2001) 'Summarising intended outcomes for older people at assessment', in H. Qureshi (ed) *Outcomes in social care practice*, Report 7, York: Social Policy Research Unit, University of York.

69 Raynes, R., Temple, B., Glenister, G. and Coulthard, L. (2001) *Quality at home for older people: Involving service users in defining home care specifications*, Bristol: The Policy Press.

70 Evans, C. and Carmichael, A. (2002) *Users' best value: A guide to user involvement good practice in best value reviews*, York: Joseph Rowntree Foundation.

71 Nicholas, E. (2001) 'Implementing an outcomes approach in carer assessment and review', in H. Qureshi (ed) *Outcomes in social care practice*, York: Social Policy Research Unit, University of York, pp 65–117.

72 Nicholas, E. (2003) 'An outcomes focus in carer assessment and review: value and challenge', *British Journal of Social Work*, vol 33, no 1, pp 31–47.

73 Bamford, C. (2001) 'Using postal questionnaires to collect information on outcomes from users and carers', in H. Qureshi (ed) *Outcomes in social care practice*, Report 7, York: Social Policy Research Unit, University of York.

[74] Clark, H. (2006) '"It's meant that, well, I'm living a life now": older people's experiences of direct payments', in J. Leece and J. Bornat (eds) *Developments in direct payments*, Bristol: The Policy Press.

[75] Patmore, C. (2001) 'Briefing sheet for home care staff: a method for focusing service around each individual user', in H. Qureshi (ed) *Outcomes in social care practice*, Report 7, York: Social Policy Research Unit, University of York.

[76] Glendinning, C., Hardy, B., Hudson, B. and Young, R. (2002) *National evaluation of notifications for use of the Section 31 partnership flexibilities in the 1999 Health Act: Final project report*, Leeds/Manchester: Nuffield Institute for Health/NPCRDC.

[77] Dowling, B., Powell, M. and Glendinning, C. (2004) 'Conceptualising successful partnerships', *Health and Social Care in the Community*, vol 12, no 4, pp 309–317.

[78] Department of Health (2006) *Modernising adult social care: Research initiative Newsletter 2*, London, DH, April.

[79] Bruce, E., Surr, C. and Tibbs, M.A. (nd) *A special kind of care: Improving well-being in people living with dementia*, Bradford Dementia Group and MHA Care Group (available at www.bradford.ac.uk/acad/health/bdg/research/methodist.php).

[80] Mackenzie, J. and Coates, D. (nd) *Understanding and supporting South Asian and Eastern European family carers of people with dementia*, Bradford Dementia Group (available at www.bradford.ac.uk/acade/health/bdg/research/supporting.php).

[81] Hudson, B., Dearey, M. and Glendinning, C. (2004) *A new vision for adult social care: Scoping service users' views*, York: Social Policy Research Unit, University of York.

Appendix 1

User involvement in the knowledge review

The User Advisory Group

In order to ensure that the knowledge review was informed by the views and experiences of older people themselves, an Advisory Group was recruited. The Advisory Group met three times during the knowledge review; each meeting was held at a point at which recent activities could be reported and immediate decisions and courses of action could be discussed and modified in the light of group discussions.

The advisory group was recruited through the Age Concern Consultation Service (ACCS). Although this is a national service, ACCS was asked to recruit up to six people from the local area (to keep down travelling costs). Other specifications were that members should be familiar with consultation activities; should have experience of using social care services; should include both women and men; should include at least two people from minority ethnic communities; and should include at least one older person with experience of caring for someone with dementia. The actual members of the group included three women and three men, two minority ethnic older people and one man whose wife had dementia and was living in a residential care home. The others all had personal experience of using social care and voluntary sector services; some had been actively involved in a Better Government for Older People pilot project; and some had taken part in previous research consultation groups.

First meeting June 2005

The first meeting of the Advisory Group took place in June 2005, after completion of the literature review and before the postal survey was conducted. The Group was given an outline of the project; invited to discuss the concept of 'outcomes' with reference to their everyday experiences; presented with the main findings from the literature review; and informed about the next stage of the project (the postal survey). Members of the group made the following points.

What do we mean by 'outcomes'?

- Not everyone finds it easy to think about what outcomes they want or what is possible – although skilled assessment can help with this.
- The outcome someone wants may not always be what is 'best' for them. Carers or professionals may seek different outcomes. There has to be a process of negotiation and people make trade-offs. Service providers may reduce independence by 'doing too much'.
- It is important to recognise individual needs and differences – it may be hard to meet these needs if they are relatively unusual (for example, special dietary needs).

Comments on the aims of the project

- Human relationships are more important than policy and paperwork. Services sometimes focus too much on the bureaucratic process of assessment rather than on outcomes.
- There was considerable discussion about access to services. It was important to include people who do not/cannot access services. Many older people do not ask for help – even the name 'social services' can be off-putting. Older people from minority ethnic groups also have to overcome language barriers – they often have to rely on their children to interpret, but if their children have been born in England they may not speak the community tongue. Social services could improve access by having closer links with the voluntary sector; groups such as Age Concern are more approachable but local authorities do not always provide adequate financial support for such groups.
- Service users need contact with someone who has an overall perspective, who can discuss what outcomes they might realistically expect in their individual situation. Home care staff (who are often in most frequent contact with older people) are not usually able to perform this role. Health services – particularly GPs – have a role to play as they are in touch with many older people (could the new community matrons fill this gap for those with the most complex needs?). But how closely are health and social services really working together?

There was a general consensus that agencies should share information as long as this is for the user's benefit and a suggestion that agencies should ask users' permission to do this on a routine basis.

What do we know already from the research that has been done?

- There are some important tasks that social services do not help with, for example, cleaning and gardening and taking someone shopping instead of doing their shopping for them. Clean and tidy homes and gardens are very important, especially to older women and those who are housebound and if premises look unkempt there are also security risks. Going shopping can keep the mind alert, as can help to keep up hobbies and social contacts.
- There was strong agreement about the importance of having choice and control over services.
- Outcomes of home care services are influenced by the calibre of care staff. Jobs are poorly paid and have low status, therefore there is high turnover. There is a need for more training and higher pay/status. The privatisation of many care services has increased communication problems – the person doing an assessment does not always communicate the desired outcomes to the actual service. In-house services can be more reliable for this reason. Home care is also perceived as very costly and costs can prevent people achieving their desired outcomes.
- Transport to services is a real problem.
- GPs have a key role in helping older people access social care services – sometimes people feel they are passed from one person to another.

Comments on the forthcoming postal survey

- The advisory group asked how the research team would know the answers obtained were accurate. It was explained that in some areas there would be more than one respondent, so answers could be cross-checked. In the six case study areas, the research team would be talking to older people and carers as well as professionals; it would be very important to find out if the 'outcomes focus' really works from the users' perspective.

- Group members were concerned the study should reach non-users of services as many older people find it hard to get information about services, especially if they are house-bound, have language difficulties or are no longer in touch with a wide range of contacts through work.

Second meeting September 2005

At this meeting, the concept of outcomes was discussed again; the preliminary results of the postal survey were presented; and plans for the case study site visits were discussed. Group members made the following points.

Further discussion of outcomes and services

- Many older people have a chronic illness and would benefit from on-going contact with a GP. However many GPs do not now visit people's homes routinely even though it can be difficult for people to attend the surgery. If someone is under the care of a consultant, some GPs can ignore their responsibility for the wider effects of the illness – for example, on the patient's mental health – and this can affect their desired outcomes from social care services.
- Current trends mean it can be difficult to get to see the same GP and shorter appointments add to the problem of having to 'start again' each time with a different GP. Lack of continuity is a potential problem for achieving an outcomes-focused approach, since changes in people's needs and desired outcomes are not tracked and discussed over time.
- Healthy eating advice and information is needed for older people to maintain their quality of life. With the right training, this could be offered by home carers.
- Being supported to get out and about (for example to go shopping and other social contacts) is important for maintaining quality of life. Without these sorts of activities, older people can become withdrawn and feel less confident and positive about life. Voluntary sector schemes to help with mobility are important, such as Dial-a-Ride;

Age Concern also offer volunteers to help people who use wheelchairs get about town to do their shopping.
- Older people feel vulnerable when they need to depend on others, especially if they do not deliver services as expected.

Preliminary results from the postal survey

- The response rate was felt to be disappointing, although perhaps not surprising and possibly reflected the low priority given to outcomes for older people.
- More services need to be encouraged to involve older people and to monitor and evaluate their outcomes-focused work, judging by the low number of organisations reporting that they currently do so.

Plans for the case study site visits – site selection

- The selection of local authorities where there was good practice was questioned – why not include a locality where things are not going so well? It was explained that it was difficult to learn anything from these sites to pass on to other areas; other bodies were responsible for identifying poorly performing local authorities; and the researchers would be asking local managers how they had overcome any problems and barriers – these lessons should help managers in other areas.
- The exclusion of a small unitary authority like York was questioned – it was explained that this was because none of these authorities who responded to the postal questionnaire had made sufficient progress with an outcomes approach to be selected as a case study site.

Plans for the case study site visits – interviews with service users

Group members made many practical suggestions about the information that service users taking part in the case study interviews and discussions would need to know before agreeing to take part. This included:

- Why did you choose me?
- What is the project about?
- How much time will it take?

- How private is it – will any staff be present?
- Can I have someone with me (for example, a friend or family member)?
- Is the information I give the researchers confidential?
- Will what I say affect any services I receive?
- Will transport be provided to the interview venue?
- Will an interpreter be available if I want someone?
- What if I look after someone else? Can the researchers cover the cost of their care while I am being interviewed?
- What feedback will I get afterwards (for example, a summary of the local case study)?

Plans for the case study site visits – questions to be asked of service users and managers

Members commented in detail on the draft topic guides for the interviews and discussion groups with older people using services in the case study sites and made many suggestions about amending the wording to make this more consistent with the experiences and concerns of older people. They suggested the following questions should be included in the interviews with service managers:

- If it was your mother receiving the service, would you be happy?
- Are you working with voluntary organisations?
- To what extent do social services share information with other relevant services or departments, for example, housing?
- How far do government policies make a difference to what actually happens in practice (not just what is on paper)?
- If an assessment identifies an outcome that cannot be met by social care services, how is that dealt with? Is it referred to another department, service or voluntary organisation?

Third meeting January 2006

The main focus of this meeting was the preliminary results from the case study site interviews. The Advisory Group was reminded of the sites and services involved and the range of staff and service users who had been interviewed. The impact of 'outcomes-focused' services in the six sites was illustrated through six 'vignettes' of service users who the researchers had met; these vignettes were intended to illustrate how different services could help people achieve change outcomes, maintenance outcomes and process outcomes.

General points about outcomes and local services

- Some Advisory Group members had received a letter from the council telling them there would be changes in their home care service but giving few concrete details. There was a rumour that all or most home care services would soon be provided by private agencies – this made people anxious, as they felt they would have less control over quality, reliability and cost. Service users were not sure if, or how, agency staff are vetted and they felt safer with the in-house service. They feel agency staff can be too young and inexperienced, and there is less continuity. If they have to use a private agency, they would prefer not to have to choose which one themselves. Older people can find it hard to be assertive, especially if they are on their own. Choice can be meaningless in such circumstances – to make it meaningful, people must have access to support and information.
- There was discussion of the planned closure of the local NHS Elderly Mentally Infirm unit. Older people were felt to have little control over such decisions, which reflect an 'ivory tower' syndrome in which such matters are decided behind closed doors.
- One advisory group member had recently received a lot of help from community nurses – he valued their company and the social aspect of their visits. He explained that people who are house-bound suffer through lack of contact with local networks that can be an important source of information.
- Another group member had been told that Housing Benefits would be paid differently in future. Again there was not much information about this and it was making people anxious.

Comments on the case study visits and 'vignettes' of service users

- When people are limited in what they can do, it can be very frustrating – this can even affect their mental health.
- The costs of home care can be an extra barrier. Private agencies are perceived as less satisfactory than in-house care.
- There was discussion about the scope of social care services and whether these included wider 'life-enhancing' outcomes such as social and leisure opportunities. The advisory group thought that this is where choice is important. It was pointed out that voluntary organisations are often able to fill these gaps, but they must have adequate funding and the flexibility to respond to individual outcomes. It was felt that some voluntary groups are now too tightly controlled by rigid contracts with their local authority.
- The individual, personalised approach was really important to users, but staff attitudes depended a lot on good training.
- Advocacy schemes – and secure funding for these – are essential in supporting older people to identify desired outcomes.

Appendix 2

Methods used in the knowledge review

Research review

The research review did not involve a systematic search for all known research. Instead it drew on published outputs from a number of recent research programmes in England and/or the UK that were known to be highly relevant to the topic. The review was restricted to the UK and to recent publications because of the difficulties of generalising from other service and policy contexts and the rapidly changing policy and practice environment in the UK.

Relevant research included:

- Outputs relating to outcomes and services for older people and their carers derived from projects carried out under the Department of Health-funded Social Policy Research Unit (SPRU) Outcomes Programme since 1996.
- The Department of Health-commissioned Outcomes of Social Care for Adults (OSCA) research programme.
- The Economic and Social Research Council's (ESRC's) Growing Older research programme.
- Recent studies carried out by the Audit Commissions's Public Sector research programme.
- Studies carried out as part of the Joseph Rowntree Foundation's programme Older People Shaping Policy and Practice.
- Research conducted as part of the Personal Social Services Research Unit (PSSRU) and Nuffield Institute of Health's Mixed Economy of Care research programme.
- Information collected by SPRU from organisations representing adult social care service users as part of a scooping exercise on their 'vision' for adult social care.[81]

This research was supplemented by a limited amount of additional searching, particularly of citations at the end of articles where these related to groups of older people who were not well represented in mainstream literature.

While this search strategy was not systematic, we are nevertheless confident that we have included all recent relevant published research. Particularly in relation to research on the outcomes desired by older people and their carers, there is a very high level of consistency between different studies, which suggests that the risk of omitting research that would significantly alter the findings of this review are relatively small.

Postal survey

Sampling framework

The contacts who were sent the postal survey were identified from a database of individuals and organisations in the UK known to have an interest in developing outcomes-focused social care services. The database was established and maintained by SPRU as part of an Outcomes Network that was set up to facilitate previous research and development work funded by the Department of Health. The database provided a broad sampling framework for what was a highly targeted survey aimed at contacts who had developed or were currently developing, outcomes-focused approaches to services for older people.

In order to identify target respondents, the database was updated to ensure that only relevant and current contacts working with older people were included in the sample to be sent the survey. Of the 340 contacts, 99 were immediately excluded because they were not in England or Wales, or were not relevant to the survey. The remaining 241 contacts were sent information about the study and a screening questionnaire in order to update the database prior to the postal survey being mailed out. Respondents to the screening questionnaire were also given the opportunity to identify other contacts, potentially unknown to the research team, within or outside their organisation, who were also developing outcomes-focused approaches to their older people's services. A reminder to complete the screening questionnaire was sent by email and/or post.

Information from responses to the screening questionnaire was used to update the database. In addition, all contact details (name, address, job title etc) of non-respondents to the postal survey were checked. The database was then used to identify the sample population for the practice survey. Sixty three contacts were excluded because they were not eligible, or because they duplicated contacts from the same organisation, or they were from NHS organisations (see below). A total sample of 222 contacts (including all non-respondents to the postal survey) was identified, including 22 contacts from Wales.

Development and content of the questionnaire

A postal questionnaire was devised. The content was informed by the research review and was designed to allow for the possibility that respondents would be engaged in a wide range of different outcomes-focused service developments, at different stages of development. A draft questionnaire was piloted with contacts in three (different) social care organisations and minor revisions were made to the questionnaire.

The questionnaire included a mix of closed and open-ended questions, with additional space for respondents to expand on their answers if they wished. Most of the questions focused on outcomes-focused work relating directly to older people, although some questions related to carers of older people, reflecting the balance of the research brief. Respondents were also encouraged to submit any supporting documents relating to the outcomes-focused activities they described in the questionnaire. The questionnaire is included in Appendix 4.

Conduct of the postal survey

A copy of the postal questionnaire together with a covering letter, information sheet about the project and freepost return address label addressed to the research team were sent to all potential respondents in July 2005. The questionnaires were pre-coded to enable respondents to be identified and not sent an unnecessary reminder. Those who had not responded within three weeks were sent a reminder, including a second copy of the questionnaire, by post. The deadline for responses was finally closed on 26 September 2005. Of the responses received, four were excluded because the respondents did not work with older people.

Data analysis

Quantitative and qualitative data from the questionnaires were entered onto an Access database, checked and verified by two of the researchers. Quantitative data were transferred to SPSS for descriptive statistical analysis. Thematic analysis of the qualitative data was carried out by the researchers, who together identified methods of categorising the data. Where supporting documents were submitted, these were logged and examined as part of the in-depth case studies (where applicable); some were also used as reference materials in subsequent work with the case study sites.

Case study sites

Initial analysis of the postal survey revealed that only six organisations in Wales had responded (including two that replied after the deadline); these were all in the early stages of developing outcomes-focused work with older people. Additional efforts were made by SCIE managers to check that these responses reflected the current state of development in Wales; their efforts confirmed the findings of the survey. As a result, the six case studies selected for more in-depth evaluation were all drawn from England on the basis that they offered the most potential for other organisations in England and Wales to learn from their experiences and practice.

Selection of case study sites

Preliminary analysis of the quantitative and qualitative data from the postal survey was conducted to identify potential case study sites. First, sites where outcomes-focused work with older people had been established for the longest period of time were identified, on the grounds that these sites would have had the greatest range of experience to draw on from which lessons for other local authorities could be learned. Seven sites reported having had outcomes-focused approaches established for more than three years. Another nine sites reported having had outcomes-focused approaches for up to three years. The remainder of the sites responding to the postal survey were in the early stages of developing their outcomes-focused work, for example, planning, rolling out, or piloting their work (including six Welsh sites that responded to the postal survey).

The 16 sites where outcomes-focused work had been established for longest were then examined in detail, together with one site from Wales that appeared to have made the most progress in developing outcomes-focused work in order to comply with the SCIE study specifications. Factors included in this analysis were: evidence of changes in assessment, care planning and/or review; developments in commissioning and/or services; multiagency working; and older people's involvement in developing outcomes-focused approaches. This analysis resulted in a 'long list' of 10 potential case study sites being identified. Among these, six sites appeared to have had an emphasis on outcomes-focused assessment, care planning and review, with the remaining four concentrating on outcomes-focused commissioning and/or service change. From this list, six preferred case study sites were selected that included both types of outcomes-focused activities; a geographical spread; and a mix of different services.

The postal survey respondent for each potential site was then contacted by the research team, to clarify their work to date and seek agreement in principle to participate. Three potential sites (including the one in Wales) declined to take part owing to competing priorities. In an attempt to secure representation of a Welsh local authority in the study, SCIE emailed all heads of adult social services in Wales to request a volunteer replacement site, but none of those responding thought they had made sufficient progress with outcomes-focused approaches to take part. Consequently, three replacement sites were sought from the long list and their agreement to take part secured.

Defining the scope of the case study fieldwork

The research team then discussed in more detail the scope of the fieldwork with each of the six sites. In each site we wished to gain both an overview of progress with outcomes-focused services for older people and to investigate a particular type of service in more depth. The latter would act as a vehicle for examining how the local outcomes approach was working in practice, including feedback from service users about the fit with their desired outcomes. Resources allowed around six face-to-face interviews with staff (slightly more if small group discussions proved appropriate), and interviews with between 12 and 18 older service users (again individually or in small groups) in each site.

Negotiating with individual sites about which type of service to focus on resulted in some changes to our initial plans, which in turn affected the final mix of services examined across the sites in total. In particular some sites were more keen for us to look at developments in intermediate care/rehabilitation services (where they felt they had made most progress), and less keen for us to focus on 'mainstream' services such as home care (where they felt they had made less progress, despite having indicated developments in their response to the postal survey). As the study aimed to learn from the experiences of case study sites, each site's assessment of the appropriate service focus was taken seriously. In practice, during the fieldwork staff and users spoke about a range of services and so we did obtain data about other services beyond the main focus of each site visit.

The six case study sites and the main service focus in each were as follows (the names of the services are those used by the site):

Case study site	Service focus in fieldwork visit
City of Bradford Metropolitan District Council	Day care
Cumbria County Council	Intermediate care
Dorset County Council	Preventative services
London Borough of Hillingdon	Home care and rehabilitation
North Lincolnshire Council	Residential care
Worcestershire County Council	Rehabilitation

Further details of each site are included in Appendix 3.

Data collection

Data were collected through site visits between the beginning of November and early December 2005. Fieldwork in each site was conducted by two researchers, one of whom took the lead in liaising with the contact person in each site (details of staff and users who were interviewed are included in Appendix 3). To help ensure consistency between sites, a common topic guide was developed for users (Appendix 4) and another for staff (Appendix 4), which could be adapted to accommodate the range of postholders we encountered in each site. Individual interviews with staff or users were carried out by a single researcher, with both researchers present for any group discussions. All data collected from staff were tape-recorded. Data collected from service users were recorded through a combination of detailed note taking and tape-recording, depending on the circumstances and individual preferences of the users involved.

Following agreement on the range and focus of the fieldwork with the lead contact in each site, s/he (or their nominee) took responsibility for recruiting appropriate staff and user respondents on our behalf. Separate project information sheets were developed for staff and users. We asked that users be approached by a member of staff who knew them to ask whether they would be willing to take part, making clear that they could withdraw at any time. At this stage, users were asked for consent for their contact details to be passed on to the research team. Staff also made appointments for the researchers either to visit a service user individually, or to speak with him/her as part of a small group discussion. A reply form was returned to the research team at this stage, with the user's contact details, a note of any known social care interventions and any needs to enable him or her to take part, for example transport. Users were asked for written consent by the researcher at the time of data collection, again being reassured that they could withdraw.

In total across the six case study sites we worked with 153 respondents, 82 of whom were staff and 71 were service users. Among the staff, the majority by far were employed by social services or working in joint health and social care teams, with the remainder either employed by the NHS, the voluntary sector or the private sector.

Data analysis

Once the fieldwork visits were complete, the notes and taped material were typed in preparation for analysis. Initially the data were written up site by site, to provide a coherent local account. To ensure a consistent approach, a template was drawn up with headings derived from the SCIE brief, which the researchers used to organise their description of each site's outcomes-focused approaches and the key issues and themes arising in the data. A number of 'vignettes' of typical users and experiences of service use were included, to give a flavour of older people's situations, care services and outcomes.

Ethical and research governance issues

Ethical approval for the practice survey was obtained from the Association of Directors of Social Services (ADSS) research group. Postal survey respondents were assured that individuals and organisations would not be identified in reports of the work without their explicit consent. Potential interviewees in the case study sites were asked for their consent for their contact details to be forwarded to the research team and were again asked for written consent before the start of each interview/focus group discussion.

The SPRU Outcomes Network database of contacts included some people working in NHS organisations. However, it was not possible to include NHS staff and organisations in the postal survey because this would have required NHS ethics and research governance approval, which it was not possible to obtain within the study timetable. However, responses to the postal survey revealed that a number of local authorities were involved in joint outcomes-focused service developments together with local NHS partners, for example, around hospital discharge and the Single Assessment Process (SAP) (England)/Unified Assessment Process (UAP) (Wales).

Furthermore, in two of the six case study sites, social services staff were working particularly closely with colleagues in the NHS and felt it was important to obtain the latter's perspectives on the development of outcomes-focused approaches. The nature of NHS staff involvement was somewhat unusual, in that they were not the subjects of the research but rather were being asked for their perspectives on local outcomes-focused service developments. The research team therefore contacted the Central Office of Research Ethics Committees (COREC) to seek guidance on whether the project needed NHS ethical approval. COREC advised that, given the nature of the project, it did not need to be submitted to an NHS research ethics committee.

In both areas in which NHS staff were involved in outcomes-focused services the researchers then contacted the local NHS research governance coordinator and research ethics committee coordinator to advise them about the project and, following advice from COREC, to clarify whether there were any local procedures that should be followed. Both the local research ethics committee coordinators accepted the COREC advice and no further action was needed. In one area the research governance coordinator required an NHS research and development application form to be completed so that they had a record of the research; in the other area the coordinator simply advised that management approval for staff involvement should be obtained from the NHS trust.

In addition, three of the social services departments involved had their own local research governance procedures. In each of these areas we completed the necessary forms and local approval for the project was given.

Appendix 3

Summary of case study sites: services and activities

This appendix contains details of the six localities included in the case study visits.

Dorset

Dorset is a predominantly rural shire county with a population of almost 400,000 – this is expected to grow by some 35 per cent in the next 25 years. Besides the county council, there are six district/borough councils and more than 20 large town and parish councils. Bournemouth and Poole have unitary authorities, which provide all services in their respective areas.

Dorset has the highest elderly population in the country (approximately 93,700), as many people choose to retire there – and it also has high life expectancy. However, funding for services for older people in Dorset is the lowest in the country – around £12 million below the average.

The Audit Commission assessed the county council as an 'excellent' authority in 2002, and the social care and health directorate (SC&H) is a two-star department. Dorset SC&H and its health partners have signed up to the innovations forum, in which the government and top-rated councils can promote new ways of working. Dorset is also piloting a local area agreement. Both initiatives are focusing on the reduction of avoidable admissions to hospital for older people and the promotion of wellbeing.

In its response to the postal survey, Dorset identified a number of areas in which it was taking forward an outcomes approach, including community and residential services, pre-and post-discharge support, day care and carers support. The case study investigation in Dorset focused on its preventative and rehabilitation services for older people; and on how services have been commissioned and developed. Services discussed and/or visited included: low-level preventative services, community re-habilitation schemes, 'home from hospital' schemes and day centres.

The case study site visit had two main strands:

- interviews (single or paired) with staff involved in developing, commissioning or managing outcomes focused approaches in preventative or rehabilitation services
- interviews and a group discussion with users of an integrated day service.

Those interviewed for the case study were staff (n=14) from social services, NHS services and voluntary organisations; service users (n=10) from day centres and user forums.

Cumbria

Cumbria is a rural county, covering an area of around 2,600 square miles. It has a population of almost 500,000, of which nearly 25 per cent are aged 60 or over. Service provision to those in the most remote communities is a challenge for both health and social care services. Cumbria Social Services works in three localities – West Cumbria, East Cumbria and South Lakeland – which reflect this spread of population.

Cumbria County Council had only one-star under comprehensive performance assessment (CPA) but is 'improving well'. In 2005, the Commission for Social care Inspection (CSCI) gave Cumbria Social Services a one-star rating (in 2003 and 2004 it had no stars), so in recent years the department has had a strong focus on improving its performance indicators.

Cumbria was chosen as a case study partly because of the work reported in the postal survey on outcomes-focused assessment and care planning. However, in the course of the case study visit it emerged that the department was about to pilot a number of significant changes in its system for contracting for home care services, which were designed to facilitate a more outcomes-focused approach. In addition, interviews with operational staff and service users focused on intermediate care services that have been developed jointly with NHS partners.

Those interviewed for the case study were: staff/managers (n=20) from social services and NHS services;10 older people who had used intermediate care services within the preceding two months. Two further interviews had been arranged but the older people concerned subsequently withdrew.

Bradford

The City of Bradford Metropolitan District Council covers Bradford, Bingley, Keighley and Shipley. It has a population of around 480,000 of which approximately 16 per cent are aged 65 and over. The population is very mixed. In the 2001 Census, 19 per cent described themselves as Asian or Asian British and 1.5 per cent as of mixed heritage. In the Indices of Deprivation 2004, Bradford was ranked at 30 out of 354 local authorities in England.

For the last three years Bradford's adult services have received a two-star rating; CSCI describes its capacity for improvement as 'promising'. In 2005 the department was successful in its application for funding for a Partnerships for Older People Pilot (POPP) project to develop integrated services for older people with mental health problems.

Bradford was one of the local authorities involved in the original SPRU outcomes research. It was chosen as a case study for the SCIE Practice Review because of its work on developing an outcomes-focused approach to assessment, care planning and review, including changes to documentation. The case study work also focused on Bradford's day care services and two facilities were visited. Both were combined residential home and day centres.

Those who took part in the study were: managers/staff (n=12) from social services; service users (n=21), including users of day care and residential care services.

Hillingdon

Hillingdon is one of the 33 London boroughs. Its population of almost a quarter of a million residents lives in about 100,000 households. Hillingdon is ranked 166 out of 354 authorities in the Indices of Deprivation 2004, but while several of its wards are among the least deprived in England, others are among the most deprived. Four fifths of the population of Hillingdon are white; Asian (mainly Punjabi) residents make up the second largest ethnic group.

The proportion of pensioner households varies across the borough from less than one per cent to 16.2 per cent. Hillingdon currently provides support to over 3,000 older people to help them live at home - above average for outer London boroughs.

The 2002 joint SSI/Audit Commission Review and the 2004 CSCI inspection identified the authority's approach as old-fashioned and called for greater clarity between the functions of in-house and independent home care providers. The CSCI report stated that 'Although the range of services was increasing, and several were delivered on a joint basis, many of the services for older people were traditional, delivered by a single agency, lacked focus on outcomes for the service user and reliant on residential and nursing home care.' These reviews, together with the appointment of a new director of social services, were the catalyst for a major reorganisation of services that have already resulted in a two-star rating (up one star) for Hillingdon's social care services for children and adults from CSCI in December 2005. Its capacity for improving its adult services is now rated as 'promising', whereas previously it was rated as 'uncertain'.

In its response to the postal survey, Hillingdon identified the following areas in which it has been developing an outcomes focus: home care; pre-discharge and post-discharge support; and day care. The case study site visit focused primarily on the commissioning and development of services which aim to (a) prevent admission to hospital or residential care or (b) rehabilitate people after hospital discharge. These included:

- rehabilitation services provided in private care homes
- the recently modernised in-house home care service
- an integrated, hospital-based (rapid response) service
- social services' community rehabilitation team.

Those interviewed for the case study included: staff ($n=17$) from social services and rehabilitation services; ten service users, most of whom had used an intermediate care facility, and some who had used home care services.

Worcestershire

Worcestershire County Council covers a mixed urban/rural area including six district councils. According to the 2001 Census, the proportion of older people was 19.1 per cent, around average for England and Wales (19 per cent). In the December 2005 CSCI assessment, Worcestershire Social Services was awarded three stars. The council has also been successful in bidding for a POPPs project.

Worcestershire returned three questionnaires in the SPRU postal survey: on its recent development of a commissioning strategy for older people's services; on its current review of the care management process for adults; and on the development of outcomes-based contract specifications for a range of new preventive services. After initial discussions with staff, it was agreed that the case study would focus on the reablement service, since this was where staff felt that they had made most progress with regard to an outcomes-based approach and therefore where most learning could be passed on.

There were three elements to the reablement service in north Worcestershire, all of which are time-limited:
* A 'next step' rehabilitation unit: in a residential and resource centre
* A residential intermediate care centre
* A community reablement team.

As well as the detailed focus on Worcestershire's reablement service, the site visit also obtained information about the development of the commissioning strategy for older people's services, the review of the care management process, and outcomes-based contract specifications for new preventive Services. While these outcomes-focused developments shared some common drivers, the sense was of separate developments as opposed to an overarching strategy for developing an outcomes-based approach across all services.

People interviewed: staff ($n=11$) from social services, PCT and voluntary sector organisations; service users ($n=12$) from reablement and intermediate care services.

North Lincolnshire

North Lincolnshire Council is a unitary authority covering a mixed urban/rural area. Twenty per cent of residents are of pensionable age – just over the average for England and Wales (19 per cent). At the time of the fieldwork, North Lincolnshire had just been successful in its bid for POPPs funding.

North Lincolnshire returned two questionnaires in the SPRU postal survey, both of which referred to changes in care management and one also drew attention to a local quality development scheme for residential and nursing homes. After initial discussions with staff, it was agreed that the case study would focus on residential care. We also obtained evidence about progress with other outcomes-focused work, in particular care management and home care.

The study team visited three residential homes (one in-house and two privately owned).

People interviewed: staff ($n=8$) from social services and residential homes; service users ($n=8$) from all three residential homes.

Appendix 4

Data collection and project documents

Postal survey of outcomes-focused services for older people

Social Policy Research Unit, University of York

Instructions for completing questionnaire

Please complete as many questions as possible. There is space at the end of the questionnaire for you to add any comments. We would be grateful for any documents (reports, plans, non-confidential minutes) that you can send us that describe outcomes-focused initiatives or practice in your organisation.

All responses to the questionnaire will be treated in confidence. Individuals and services will not be identified in reports of the survey. However, we would like to identify a small number of localities where we can look in detail at innovative outcomes-focused approaches to older people's services. We would therefore be grateful if you could give us your contact details. Names and/or localities would only be identified with the permission of those concerned

For the purposes of this survey, the terms below are defined as follows:

- *Outcomes* – the impact, effect or consequence of help received from services.
- *Outcomes-focused approaches* – ways of organising services so that they can achieve the outcomes that service users desire.
- *Older people* – service users aged 65+.
- *Services* – social services and their partner organisations/agencies (for example, health, voluntary services) involved in outcomes-focused work.

If you are not involved in any outcomes-focused work with older people, please only complete questions 1-3.

If you have any queries or need any help completing the questionnaire, please contact Janet Heaton (jh35@york.ac.uk; tel: 01904 321950) or Caroline Glendinning (cg20@york.ac.uk; tel: 01904 321951).

Please return the questionnaire within two weeks using the FREEPOST label provided.

Os dymunwch gael copi o'r holiadur hwn yn Gymraeg wnewch chi roi gwybod i ni os gwelwch yn dda.

If you would like a copy of this questionnaire in Welsh please let us know.

Part A: You and your organisation

1. Please provide your name and contact details

Title: Mr ☐   Miss ☐   Ms ☐   Mrs ☐   Dr ☐   Other ☐

(please specify)..

First name: ....

Surname:..

Job title: ....

Name of organisation you work in:..................................

....

Address:..

Postcode: ....

Tel: ....

Email: ....

2. What type of organisation(s) do you work in?

(Please tick all that apply)

Local authority/social services	☐
PCT	☐
NHS trust	☐
Voluntary organisation	☐
Private service provider	☐
Private consultancy	☐
Other (please state)	☐

3. Which of the following service user groups does your job include?

(Please tick all that apply)

Older people aged 65+	☐
Other	☐

If you answered only 'Other' to Q3, there is no need to complete any more questions. But please return the questionnaire in the envelope provided (so that we know how many people we contacted are not doing work with older people and their carers). Thank you.

Part B: Involvement in outcomes-focused work for older people

4. Are you involved in any of the following outcomes-focused approaches to older people's services?

(Please tick all that apply)

Planning services that aim to identify and achieve the outcomes ☐
valued by older people

Commissioning services that aim to identify and achieve the ☐
outcomes valued by older people

Providing services that aim to identify and achieve the outcomes ☐
valued by older people

Monitoring and evaluating effectiveness of outcomes-focused ☐
services for older people

Involving older people in the design and development of ☐
outcomes-focused services

Independent consultancy/development work with social care ☐
services

Other type of outcomes-focused work for older people ☐

Outcomes-focused approaches to supporting carers of older people ☐

If you have answered 'No' to ALL items in Q4, there is no need to complete any more questions. But please return the questionnaire in the envelope provided (so that we know how many people we contacted are not doing work with older people). Thank you.

5. Please briefly describe the nature of the outcomes-focused approaches to older people's services in your organisation. (Please supply any related documents describing this work when you return the questionnaire.)

6. Which of the following best describes the stage of development of the outcomes-focused work you described in Q5?

Established in practice for more than three years ☐
Established in practice for three years or less ☐
Currently being 'rolled-out' ☐
Currently being piloted ☐
In planning stages ☐
Other (please describe) ☐

....

....

Part C: Service organisation and partnerships

7. Does the outcomes-focused approach(es) you have described to older people's services involve any other organisations?

No, this department only ☐ (Please go to Q8)
Yes ☐
If **Yes**, is this joint with ...:
(Please tick all that apply)
Local authority/social services ☐
PCT ☐
NHS trust ☐
Voluntary organisation ☐
Private – service provider ☐
Private – consultancy ☐
Other (please state) ☐ ....

If joint, which is the lead agency?
(Please tick one only)
Local authority/social services ☐
PCT ☐
NHS trust ☐
Voluntary organisation ☐
Private – service provider ☐
Private – consultancy ☐
Other (please state type of organisation) ☐ ....
No single lead agency ☐

Part D: Older people

8. Please tell us which of the following groups of older people are covered by your outcomes-focused approach(es) to older people's services.

(Please tick all that apply)

a) Older people living at home

    Yes ☐

    No ☐

    Don't know ☐

b) Older people living in residential care

    Yes ☐

    No ☐

    Don't know ☐

c) Older people in hospital prior to discharge

    Yes ☐

    No ☐

    Don't know ☐

d) Older people immediately after discharge from hospital

    Yes ☐

    No ☐

    Don't know ☐

e) Older people attending day care

    Yes ☐

    No ☐

    Don't know ☐

f) Older people with dementia

    Yes ☐

    No ☐

    Don't know ☐

g) Older people from black and/or minority ethnic groups

    Yes ☐

    No ☐

    Don't know ☐

h) Carers of older people

    Yes ☐

    No ☐

    Don't know ☐

Part E: Approaches to outcomes-focused work

9. Which of the following activities does your outcomes-focused approach(es) to older people's services involve?
(Please tick all that apply)
a) Identifying outcomes desired by individual older people at assessment
Yes – currently for most/all ☐
Yes – currently for some ☐
Yes – still at planning stage ☐
No ☐
N/A ☐
Don't know ☐

b) A focus on outcomes in care planning for older people
Yes – currently for most/all ☐
Yes – currently for some ☐
Yes – still at planning stage ☐
No ☐
N/A ☐
Don't know ☐

c) Reviewing whether outcomes desired by individual older people at assessment are achieved
Yes – currently for most/all ☐
Yes – currently for some ☐
Yes – still at planning stage ☐
No ☐
N/A ☐
Don't know ☐

d) Commissioning/developing brand new services to better meet older people's needs and preferences

Yes – currently for most/all	☐
Yes – currently for some	☐
Yes – still at planning stage	☐
No	☐
N/A	☐
Don't know	☐

e) Changing existing services to better meet older people's needs and preferences

Yes – currently for most/all	☐
Yes – currently for some	☐
Yes – still at planning stage	☐
No	☐
N/A	☐
Don't know	☐

f) Monitoring/evaluating services to examine extent to which services are outcomes-focused for older people

Yes – currently for most/all	☐
Yes – currently for some	☐
Yes – still at planning stage	☐
No	☐
N/A	☐
Don't know	☐

10. To what extent have older people (service users) been involved in planning the above approaches?

Greatly	☐
Moderately	☐
A little	☐
Not at all	☐
Don't know	☐
N/A	☐

11. What have been the main achievements or impact of your outcomes-focused approach(es) to older people's services? (Please rank these in order of importance, where 1 is the most important achievement/impact.)

1 ....

....

2 ....

....

3 ....

....

Part F: What has helped and what has hindered you and your organisation make progress on outcomes-focused approaches to older people's services?

12. What three things have most *helped* you and your organisation progress outcomes-focused approaches to older people's services? (Please rank these in order of priority, where 1 is the most important factor.) Possible examples are: commitment of managers, policy developments, philosophy of staff, training of staff

1 ....

....

2 ....

....

3 ....

....

13. What three things have most *hindered* you and your organisation in developing outcomes-focused approaches to older people's services? (Please rank these in order of priority, where 1 is the most important factor.) Possible examples are: targets, resources, workload, training of staff

1 ....

....

2 ....

....

3 ....

....

14. Have you taken any measures to overcome the barriers you mentioned in Q13?

No   ☐

Yes (Please describe):   ☐ ....

....

....

15. If you answered 'Yes' to Q14, were they successful?

Yes – fully ☐
Yes – partly ☐
No ☐
Too early to say ☐
Don't know ☐
Not applicable ☐

> Please use the space at the end of the questionnaire for any additional comments.

Instructions for returning questionnaire

Please return the questionnaire using the FREEPOST label provided.

Please remember to enclose any documents describing the outcomes projects or service developments you are involved in.

If you have any queries or need help completing the questionnaire, please contact Janet Heaton (jh35@york.ac.uk; tel 01904 321950) or Caroline Glendinning (cg20@york.ac.uk; tel 01904 321951).

What happens next

We will analyse the responses to this questionnaire and write a report on the range of outcomes-focused approaches to services for older people. The report will be included in the knowledge review that SPRU will prepare for SCIE.

We also wish to follow up a small number of localities and investigate in more detail their outcomes-focused approaches to older people's services. We may therefore contact you again to ask if your organisation would be willing to participate in this more detailed study, which will take place during the autumn 2005.

Please use the space below to add any additional comments you wish.

Thank you for completing the questionnaire.

Practice survey of outcomes-focused services for older people

Social Policy Research Unit, University of York with Acton Shapiro

Case study sites

Topic guide for service users – general

1. Introductory questions

What kind of services are you using? How long have you been using them?

> "In many areas, services are quite restricted and can't necessarily take into account the different lifestyles and preferences of individual older people. What we are really interested in is finding out whether the services you get help you to live the sort of life you want. That might be about helping you just to keep going, for example, helping you to keep clean and tidy and safe, or to keep in touch with other people. Or it could be about helping things to change or improve, for example, by becoming more independent. And it's also about how much control and choice you feel you have about how things are done."

2. Your outcomes

Thinking about yourself, what is it that really matters to you in how you live your life? *[prompt and probe against standard list of outcomes valued by older people]*
Probes:

- Is there anything you might want to change or improve?
- What about the emotional and social aspects of your life, as well as the practicalities?

3. Your assessment

How much do you feel you have been encouraged to think and talk about what really matters to you when services have been set up? Or were you just told what you could have?

- How easy did you find it to do this?
- How easy do you think your assessor found it to talk in terms of your own priorities (rather than just about services)?
- How often do you get the chance to talk about how well things are working or whether you would like something to change?

4. Your services

On a day-to-day basis, do you feel the services you are getting are helping you to live the kind of life you want?

- What's working well, what is not?
- How well do you feel your services work together?
- How much day-to-day choice and control do you feel you have over what services you get and how they are delivered (for example, timing, what is done, who by) – or are these restricted?
- Do you feel you are treated with respect?
- Do you have any cultural or religious preferences relating to services? If so, do services take account of these?
- Have you got anyone else helping you (family, neighbour?) If so, do services try to fit in with what they do?
- Do you pay for any of your social care services? If so, do you feel they are good value for money?

5. General questions

Overall, how good are services at helping you live the life you want?

Over time, have they been getting better at doing this?

On reflection, do you think other areas can learn anything from how things are done here?

Outcomes-focused social services for older people

A review for the Social Care Institute for Excellence (SCIE)

Topic guide for service users in care homes/other residential settings

Name: Date: Interviewer: Age:

Preliminaries

1. Show ID card/ thanks for taking part/check end time OK

2. Purpose of study:

* Across England and Wales, social services departments are being encouraged to make sure that the services they set up provide help with
  the things that older people themselves say are important to them.
* The overall aim of the project is to see what progress is being made
  – we are doing this in three ways: by looking at research already carried
  out; by sending a questionnaire to social services departments across
  England and Wales asking them to let us know what they are doing;
  and by visiting in person six local 'case study' areas, including *[local
  case study site]*, to learn from the progress you are making locally.
* The Social Care Institute for Excellence has asked for the project to
  be done to find out what lessons can be learned for everyone.
* We want to talk to staff and people like yourself who have been using services, to ask about what is working well and what is difficult
  in making sure that services are helping with the things that are
  important for older people such as yourself.
* We will write a report based on what you and other people and staff
  tell us, but no one's names will be mentioned – what we discuss is
  private.

3. Area of special service interest

* One of the reasons we decided to come to *[local case study site]* was to
  find out in particular what has been happening in relation to *[area*

of special service interest]. So we asked to speak to you in particular because you have had experience of that service.

- But we don't want to limit the discussion to that service because we are also interested in any other social services help you receive (eg home care, day care etc) because what's important most of all is how services together are helping you to live the life you want.
- Of course, as researchers, we can't ourselves influence the services you get. But what you tell us can be used to help improve the way things are done here and in other areas.

4. Any questions?

5. Happy to take part?

- Ask person to complete consent form.

6. Seek agreement to take notes/tape-record the interview

7. Don't have to answer any questions you don't want to, and can stop any time for whatever reason.

QUESTIONS

To begin: Can you tell me a little about your circumstances at the moment.... Are you a resident here, or using day care, intermediate care (rehab), respite, short stay (for example, for assessment) etc?

Residents: How long have you been here? How did you come to this [home]? Did you have a choice of other places? What made you choose this place? Does it suit you?

Others: How did you come to be getting [service] here? How long have you been here for [service]? Did you have an assessment before you came? Were you getting any help from social services before you came here?

2. What matters to you

2.1 We're interested to find out how services are helping you. So, thinking about yourself, what is it that really matters to you in how you live your life?
Residents: How do you spend your time here? What do you like to do? Do you have any special interests or hobbies? Do you like socialising or prefer your own company? Are you able to do these things as much as you would like/live your life as you please?

Others: How do you spend your time here? What do you want to get out of the service while you're here? [*for example, social contact with people; become more independent; be able to take care of self so able to stay at home*]

2.2 Is there anything you might want to change or improve in your life? If so, what could be done to enable that?

2.3 *[if not mentioned]* What about the emotional and social aspects of your life, as well as the practicalities?

3. Services/help

What kind of services are you using/ help are you getting? [*for each service]* how long has this been in place?

Residents: Do you need any help from people to get around or do things (eg look after yourself)? What kind of help do you need? Are you getting enough help with [ ]? Who provides that help (for example, the home, or outside services for example, own GP)? Do you have a keyworker? If so, do you talk to her about your needs and preferences?

Others: What help are you getting while you're here? Do you need help with getting around or doing things (eg looking after yourself)? Are you getting enough help with [ ]?

4. Your assessment

How much do you feel you have been encouraged to think and talk about what really matters to you while you've been here/when your services were set up? *[Or were you just told what you could have?]*

Residents: Has anyone encouraged you to think and talk about what matters to you and done something about it? Or were you just told what was on offer? *[for example, food choices, range of social events/activities on offer]*

Others: Has anyone encouraged you to think and talk about what matters to you while you've been here? … or before you came here?

[If yes] How easy did you find it to do this?

[If applicable] How easy do you think your [keyworker]/assessor found it to talk in terms of your own wishes/priorities (rather than just about services)?

5. Your services

We're interested to know, on a day-to-day basis, whether you feel the care and support [services] you are getting is helping you to live the kind of life you want.…

What is working well?

Can you give me an example of how the help you get here has made [or might make] a positive difference to your life? *[Or an example from the help you've had before?]*

What is not working so well?

Is there any aspect of your life where you are not getting the help that you would like? If so, what could be done to make that better?

How often do you get the chance to talk about how well things are working or whether you would like something to change (for example, do you get a regular review)?

What would you do if you were not happy about any aspect of your service(s)?

How well do you feel the care and support [services] work together here?

How much day-to-day choice and control do you feel you have over what services you get and how they are delivered *[for example, timing, what is done, who by]* – or are these restricted?

Do you feel you are treated with respect?

Do you have any cultural or religious preferences relating to services? If so, do services take account of these?

Have you got anyone else helping you (family, friends, neighbour?) If so, do services try to fit in with what they do?

Do you pay for any of your social care services? If so, do you feel they are good value for money?

6. General questions

Overall, how good are services at helping you live the life you want?

Over time, have they been getting better at doing this?

What do you think other parts of the country could learn from how things are done here?

Closure

What happens next

We will write up our notes from the six areas across the country we are visiting in a report, along with the other aspects of the research we have already done. No names will be used in the report so no one will know exactly who said what. *Check as appropriate that the person is happy for us to use all the material.*

Our report will be sent to the Social Care Institute for Excellence, who will use it to write a practical 'resource guide' next year to help all local authorities.

Any questions?

Thanks.

Practice survey of outcomes-focused services for older people

Social Policy Research Unit, University of York with Acton Shapiro

Topic guide for managers (care managers, commissioners, providers)

Name:	Date:	Interviewer:

Opening points for interviewer

- Thanks the interviewee for agreeing to take part in the review
- Explain how the material from the review will be used
- Reassure them about confidentiality
- Ask if there is anything else they would like to know about the review
- Use the definition below if asked for one.

NB: Outcomes-focused approaches are those which 'promote and develop services designed to identify and achieve the outcomes (that is, lifestyle or quality of life) that older people desire'.

Section 1: Introductory questions

*1.1   Can you briefly describe your role?

*1.2   What was the initial motivation behind developing an outcomes-based approach? What specific benefits were anticipated? *[check user benefits covered]*

*1.3   *[for managers with a strategic overview]* Can you briefly describe how your local outcomes approach has been developed and implemented?

Or *[for those with knowledge of part of the process]* How have you been involved in developing an outcomes-based approach locally?

Prompt for: Any challenges in relation to particular services

Which partner agencies have been involved and how this has helped/hindered

*1.4   What did you draw on to help you? *[for example, SPRU pack; training; research articles; meetings with local organisations; experiences from other areas]*

*1.5   To what extent have current policy priorities and requirements helped or hindered the development of an outcomes approach? *[for example, NSF for older people, FACS, SAP, performance management regimes and targets, health flexibilities]*

*1.6   To what extent have older people and their carers been involved (at a collective level) in developing your outcomes approach? *[Prompt for: what difference any involvement has made]*

Section 2: Core Questions

For some managers (for example, in service management/provider roles) we will be asking them to think about a specific *area of work [agreed in advance with the case study area]:*

- home care
- day care
- intermediate care or rehabilitation services
- residential care.

Questions for case study areas where the focus has been on *assessment, care planning, care management and review*

*2.1   Can you tell us specifically what changes have been made to implement an outcomes approach *[cover the following separately: assessment, care planning, care management and review?]*

*2.2   What local factors have helped or hindered your progress so far?

2.3   a) How easy has it been for you and your colleagues to think and talk to older people and carers in terms of outcomes rather than services?

b) What steps (if any) have been taken to achieve the change in culture? [*Prompt for: how effective any initiatives have been; what as worked well/less well; what have been the most difficult issues/areas to address?*]

2.4 Do you feel you have been able to achieve an holistic approach that is, one that includes process outcomes and emotional and-social outcomes, as well as practical ones

2.5 How much freedom do care managers have to purchase/coordinate the services older people need to achieve their outcomes? [*prompt for example of a challenging one*]

2.6 How have you and your colleagues addressed any tensions between risk management and outcomes?

2.7 How have you managed to balance outcomes for carers with those for users?

2.8 How easy have older people and carers found it to talk to you in terms of how they want to live their lives?

2.9 Have older people and their carers been involved (at an individual level) in key decisions about services that are important to them (for example, about the choice of provider)?

2.10 How much control do you feel older people have over their day-to-day services and how these are delivered (for example, timing, what is done, who by)?

2.11 Have there been any particular challenges in identifying and addressing outcomes for specific individuals or user groups [*for example, people with dementia; people from black and minority ethnic communities?*]

2.12 Has the outcomes approach in assessment and care planning been matched by new ways of commissioning, contracting and developing services?

Questions for case study areas where the focus has been on *commissioning, planning, service development and provision*
*2.13 How you have commissioned/developed services to achieve older people's outcomes?

Prompt for: Balance between changes to existing services and creation of new services

2.14　How have partnerships changed or developed?

2.15　What changes have you made to your contracts?

2.16　Have there been other changes in the way commissioners and providers relate to each other (for example, communication, payment methods)?

*2.17　What local factors have helped or hindered your progress so far?

2.18　How are you ensuring a common understanding of your outcomes approach between commissioners, care managers, provider agencies and front-line staff?

2.19　How are you ensuring that other agencies understand your outcomes approach (for example, housing, leisure, health, voluntary organisations)?

2.20　Have providers needed to change their organisational arrangements (for example, how they recruit, deploy and pay staff, what tasks they are allowed to do)?

2.21　Through your new contracts, have you been able to support the relationship between older people and their front-line worker(s) (for example, through facilitating time to socialise; continuity of staff)?

2.22　How much control do you feel older people have over their day-to-day services and how these are delivered (for example, timing, what is done, who by)?

2.23　How have you and your colleagues addressed any tensions between risk management and outcomes?

2.24　Do you feel you have been able to achieve a holistic approach that is, one that includes emotional and social outcomes, as well as practical ones?

2.25　Has the outcomes approach in commissioning, contracting and developing services been matched by new ways of assessment, care planning and review?

Section 3: Training, monitoring and evaluation

*3.1   Can you tell me about the training that has been delivered on outcomes and any lessons learnt?

Prompt for: which staff groups/organisations have been involved in the training

Whether the focus has been on culture or process

*3.2   How is the implementation of your outcomes approach being monitored?

Prompt for: what measures have been used to monitor progress

*3.3   How are you evaluating the impact on: (a) older people (b) carers (c) staff (d) resources?

*3.4   Have older people and their carers been involved in any way in evaluating the impact of your approach so far?

Prompt for: how they have been involved

What difference their involvement has made

Section 4: Overall reflections and thinking about the future

*4.1   In summary, what have been the main changes you have needed to make to the organisation and delivery of services?

*4.2   To what extent do you feel your aims have been realised? Have other benefits emerged?

*4.3   [for sites in England] How do you intend to build on existing practice to implement the proposals in the Green Paper on adult social care?

*4.4   Thinking about sustainability, what challenges do you face now in building on your initial achievements with an outcomes approach? [prompt to cover sustainability both within a service and in terms of broadening an outcomes approach to other services]

Section 5: Transferability

*5.1   If you were talking to a group of managers from another area, what would your advice be to them in taking forward an outcomes approach

Prompt for: what the critical success factors have been – explore these as fully as possible

Essential 'dos' and 'don'ts'

*5.2   From your experience, what lessons have been learned about successful joint working? *[for example, NHS, voluntary organisations, private sector – check which lessons apply to which]*

Closing points for interviewer

- Thank the interviewee for answering our questions
- Ask if there is anything they want to add
- Explain what will happen next, including likely timescales for our work and publication of SCIE guidance

Appendix 5

Information about SPRU and Acton Shapiro

Social Policy Research Unit (SPRU)

Since its establishment in 1973 at the University of York, SPRU's research has focused on children, young people and adults made vulnerable by poverty, ageing, disability or chronic illness. Most of SPRU's research falls within the broad policy areas of social security, social care and health care. SPRU has an international reputation for excellence in research.

SPRU's research is underpinned by the following principles:

- to reflect and communicate the experiences and views of the users of services and beneficiaries of policy interventions
- to recognise that people's lives do not divide into neat segments which coincide with agency and professional boundaries, and to conduct research which crosses these boundaries
- to make its research influential in bringing about change; to communicate findings effectively to key audiences; and to engage actively with policy-makers and practitioners

More information about SPRU can be found at www.york.ac.uk/spru

Acton Shapiro

Acton Shapiro is an independent company based near York which specialises in consultancy and research in the fields of health and social care. Its staff have experience in healthcare management, nursing, social care, academic research and the voluntary sector; its projects utilise a portfolio of qualitative and quantitative techniques. Acton Shapiro's core areas of work are:

- applied research, service evaluations and reviews, including local evaluation of national initiatives such as the Partnerships for Older People Project

- supporting service planning, innovation and change, including developing outcomes-focused approaches in social care
- consulting and involving, patients, carers, service users and the public.

Acton Shapiro works with local authorities, strategic health authorities, primary care trusts, individual GP practices, national and local voluntary sector organisations and multi- and inter-agency initiatives. In collaboration with academic partners, it has undertaken a number of projects for national research bodies (for example, NHS Service Delivery and Organisation R&D Programme and Joseph Rowntree Foundation) and national advisory/inspection bodies (for example, Social Care Institute for Excellence). Its focus is on finding practical solutions that work for the teams, organisations or communities involved.

More information about Acton Shapiro can be found at www.actionshapiro.co.uk

Index

A

Accelerated Development
Programme 55
activity 4–5
Acton Shapiro 127–8
Age Concern 23, 47, 57, 76
Age Concern Consultation
Service (ACCS) 75
alertness 4–5
Askham, J. 8
assessments
case studies x, 41–2
facilitating outcomes-focused
services vii, 18–19
impeding outcomes-focused
services vii, 10–11
Association of Directors of Social
Services (ADSS) 90

B

Better Commissioning Learning
and Information Network
(LIN) 26, 27
outcome-based commissioning
39, 45–6
Bradford 40, 88, 95
Butt, J. 8

C

Callaghan, G. 16
Canadian Occupational
Performance Measure 48
care packages
micro-level commissioning vii, 21

purchasing impeding outcomes-
focused services 12–13
care planning vii, x, 41–2
carers 58–9
case studies x, 25, 26, 39–41
conclusions 63
factors facilitating outcome
approaches xii, 54–7
factors hindering outcome
approaches xii, 57–9
impact of outcomes-focused
services 50–4
methods 86–91
monitoring and evaluation xii,
48–9
outcomes-focused activities x–xi,
41–7
outcomes-focused services xi–xii,
47–8
plans for (further) outcomes-
focused service developments
59–61
summary of sites 93–8
User Advisory Group 79–80, 82
Central Office of Research Ethics
Committees (COREC) 90
Centre for Policy on Ageing 42
Change Agent Team 26, 37
change management 55–6
change outcomes
commissioning case studies x, 43
experiences of service users 50–1
valued by older people vi, 3, 7
Commission for Social Care
Inspection (CSCI)

facilitating outcome approaches 37, 39, 55
hindering outcome approaches 37, 57
commissioning viii, 14–15
  case studies x–xi, 43–7
  micro-level vii, 21
communication
  facilitating outcomes-focused services 22
  impeding outcomes-focused services 15–16
contracting viii, 14–15
  case studies 43–7
control 5–7
Cumbria County Council 40, 88, 94–5

D
day care
  case studies xi, 48
  constraints on impact of outcomes-focused approaches 54
  maintenance outcomes 51–2
  process outcomes 52–3, 63
dementia 23
Department of Health 26, 84
direct payments 1
  helping and hindering progress 21, 37, 39
diversity
  and barriers to outcomes-focused services 17
facilitating outcomes-focused services 23
  outcomes valued by older people 8–9

Domiciliary Care Standards Regulations (2003) 11
Dorset County Council 40, 88, 93–4

E
environment 4
evaluation xii, 48–9

F
Fair Access to Care Services (FACS) 1, 10
  assessments 10
  case studies 42
  purchasing of care packages 12
  reviews 20
Francis, J. 21

G
Godfrey, M. 16
GPs 23, 58
Green Paper on adult social care 25, 26
  facilitating outcome approaches 39, 55
  holistic perspective 3
  personalisation 2

H
Hardy, B. 11
Health Act 1999, Section 31 1, 16, 22
health-social care divide
  facilitating outcomes-focused services 22–3
  impeding outcomes-focused services 16–17
Hillingdon 40, 88, 95–6

home care services 9–10, 64
  constraints on impact of
    outcomes-focused approaches
    54
  maintenance outcomes 51
  monitoring and evaluation 49
  organisational arrangements
    facilitating outcomes-focused
    services 18–23
  organisational arrangements
    impeding outcomes-focused
    services 9–17

I
in-house services 43
independence 2
independent providers see private
  service providers
Innovations Forum 55
intermediate care 63
  case studies x, xi, 47–8
  change outcomes 50–1
  facilitating outcome approaches
    55
  monitoring and evaluation 48
  process outcomes 52–3
  service-level outcomes 54
intermediate care services,
  constraints on impact of
  outcomes-focused approaches
  54

J
joint working see partnerships

L
leadership 55–6
Lincolnshire 40, 88, 98

local authorities 28, 29
local vision 55–6
London Borough of Hillingdon
  40, 88, 95–6

M
maintenance outcomes
commissioning case studies x–xi,
  44–7
  experiences of service users 51–2
  plans for (further) developments
    60–1
  valued by older people vi, 4–6,
    7
micro-level commissioning vii, 21
Mirza, K. 8
Modernisation Agency 55
Mold, F. 8
monitoring and evaluation xii,
  48–9
multiagency working see
  partnerships

N
national policies
  facilitating outcome approaches
    37, 54–5
  hindering outcome approaches
    37, 57
National Service Framework
  (NSF) for older people 1, 55
  assessments 10
  helping and hindering progress
    37, 39
Netten, A. 8, 21
NHS acute trusts 28, 29
Nicholas, E. 19–20

North Lincolnshire Council 40,
88, 98
Northumberland Care Trust 42
nursing homes 48

O
older people
outcomes valued 3–9
see also User Advisory Group;
users
organisational arrangements
facilitating outcomes-focused
services 18–23
impeding outcomes-focused
services 9–17
organisational change and culture
35
outcomes
definition v, 2–3
User Advisory Group 76
valued by older people v–vi,
3–9, 24
outcomes-focused activities
case studies 41–7
groups covered 30, 31
older people's involvement in
planning 31, 32
specific 31, 32
stages 28, 29
types 28, 30
outcomes-focused approaches 1
factors facilitating xii, 54–7
factors hindering xii, 57–9
outcomes-focused services
achievements 33–7
case studies xi–xii, 47–8
conclusions xiii–xv, 63–5
definition 2

experiences of service users
50–4
factors facilitating and
inhibiting vii–viii
organisational arrangements
facilitating viii–ix, 18–23, 24
organisational arrangements
impeding 9–17, 24
plans for (further) developments
59–61
see also practice survey
Outcomes of Social Care
Research and Development
Programme 25–6

P
partnerships 1, 34
facilitating outcome approaches
16, 22–3, 56–7, 64–5
postal survey 28, 29
Partnerships for Older People
Projects (POPPs) 39
Patmore, C. 14, 21–2
performance indicators 57
personal safety 4
personalisation 2
physical needs 4
postal survey ix, 25, 26
achievements and factors
helping and hindering
achievements 33–7
aims 26–7
discussion 38–9
methods 27, 84–6, 99–125
nature and range of outcomes
work 28, 29, 30–2
respondent characteristics 27–8
User Advisory Group 77–8, 79

practice survey 25–6
  conclusions 63
  ethical and research governance
    issues 90
  see also case studies; postal
    survey
prevention outcomes
  plans for (further) developments
    60–1
  valued by older people vi, 4–6,
    7
primary care trusts 28, 29
private consultancy 28, 29
private service providers
  commissioning 44–7
  postal survey 28, 29
process outcomes
  experiences of service users 52–3
  valued by older people vi, 6–7
provider-level factors vii
  facilitating outcomes-focused
    services 21–2
  impeding outcomes-focused
    services 13–14
purchasing 12–13
  micro-level vii, 21

Q
Quality Development Scheme
  (QDS) 48
quality of life 2
Qureshi, H. 3, 18–19

R
reablement services 64
  case studies xi, 47–8
  change outcomes 50–1
    monitoring and evaluation 48
    process outcomes 52–3
    service-level outcomes 54
recording systems and tools 36
research review 1, 83–4
  conclusions 24
  organisational arrangements
    facilitating outcomes-focused
      services 18–23
  organisational arrangements
    impeding outcomes-focused
      services 9–17
  outcomes valued by older people
    3–9
residential care 63
  case studies xi
  maintenance outcomes 51–2
  monitoring and evaluation 49
  outcomes-focused services 48
  process outcomes 52–3
  service-level outcomes 54
resources 36
  constraints 57–8
reviews
  case studies x, 42
  facilitating outcomes-focused
    services 19–21
  factors facilitating and
    inhibiting vii
  impeding outcomes-focused
    services 11–12

S
service process outcomes *see*
  process outcomes
service users *see* users
service-level outcomes 54

Single Assessment Process (SAP)
1, 10, 16
case studies 41–2
helping and hindering progress
37, 39
hindering outcome approaches
57, 64
reviews 20
social contact 5
Social Policy Research Unit
(SPRU) 1, 18, 127
Outcomes Network 25–6, 41,
55, 63, 84, 90
postal survey 27
social services 28, 29
staff attitudes 35, 58

T
training 34

U
Unified Assessment Process
(UAP) 37, 90
User Advisory Group xiii, 26,
75–82
case studies 40–1
organisational arrangements
facilitating outcomes-focused
services 23
organisational arrangements
impeding outcomes-focused
services 17
outcome-based commissioning
46–7
outcomes valued by older people
9
partnerships 56–7
postal survey 38

users
attitudes hindering outcome
approaches 58–9
impact of outcomes-focused
services xiii, 50–4

V
voluntary organisations 64–5
postal survey 28, 29

W
Ware, T. 16
whole systems working
change management 55–6
facilitating outcome approaches
56–7
Worcestershire County Council
40, 88, 97

Other knowledge reviews available from SCIE

LEARNING AND TEACHING IN SOCIAL WORK EDUCATION: ASSESSMENT
Beth R. Crisp, Mark R. Anderson, Joan Orme and Pam Green Lister
ISBN 1 904812 00 7
November 2003
Ordering code: KR01

THE ADOPTION OF LOOKED AFTER CHILDREN: A SCOPING REVIEW OF RESEARCH
Alan Rushton
ISBN 1 904812 01 5
November 2003
Ordering code: KR02

TYPES AND QUALITY OF KNOWLEDGE IN SOCIAL CARE
Ray Pawson, Annette Boaz, Lesley Grayson, Andrew Long and Colin Barnes
ISBN 1 904812 02 3
November 2003
Ordering code: KR03

INNOVATIVE, TRIED AND TESTED: A REVIEW OF GOOD PRACTICE IN FOSTERING
Clive Sellick and Darren Howell
ISBN 1 904812 03 1
November 2003
Ordering code: KR04

FOSTERING SUCCESS: AN EXPLORATION OF THE RESEARCH LITERATURE IN FOSTER CARE
Kate Wilson, Ian Sinclair, Claire Taylor, Andrew Pithouse and Clive Sellick
ISBN 1 904812 04 X
January 2004
Ordering code: KR05

TEACHING AND LEARNING COMMUNICATION SKILLS IN SOCIAL WORK EDUCATION
Pamela Trevithick, Sally Richards, Gillian Ruch and Bernard Moss with Linda Lines and Oded Manor
ISBN 1 904812 12 0
May 2004
Ordering code: KR06

IMPROVING THE USE OF RESEARCH IN SOCIAL CARE PRACTICE
Isabel Walter, Sandra Nutley, Janie Percy-Smith, Di McNeish and Sarah Frost
ISBN 1 904812 13 9
June 2004
Ordering code: KR07

TEACHING, LEARNING AND ASSESSMENT OF LAW IN SOCIAL WORK EDUCATION
Suzy Braye and Michael Preston-Shoot with Lesley-Ann Cull, Robert Johns and Jeremy Roche
ISBN 1 904812 20 1
April 2005
Ordering code: KR08

LEARNING AND TEACHING IN SOCIAL WORK EDUCATION: TEXTBOOKS AND FRAMEWORKS ON ASSESSMENT
Beth R. Crisp, Mark R. Anderson, Joan Orme and Pam Green Lister
ISBN 1 904812 21 x
April 2005
Ordering code: KR09

THE LEARNING, TEACHING AND ASSESSMENT OF PARTNERSHIP IN SOCIAL WORK EDUCATION
Imogen Taylor, Elaine Sharland, Judy Sebba and Pat Leriche with Elaine Keep and David Orr
ISBN 1 904812 34 1
June 2006
Ordering code: KR10

SUPPORTING DISABLED PARENTS AND PARENTS WITH ADDITIONAL SUPPORT NEEDS
Jenny Morris and Michele Wates
November 2006
Online only

TEACHING, LEARNING AND ASSESSING COMMUNICATION SKILLS WITH CHILDREN AND YOUNG PEOPLE IN SOCIAL WORK EDUCATION
Barry Luckock, Michelle Lefevre, David Orr, Mary Jones, Ruth Marchant and Karen Tanner
ISBN 1 904812 14 7
December 2006
Ordering code: KR12

For enquiries or renewal at
Quarles LRC
Tel: 01708 455011 – Extension 4009